AGAINST ALL ODDS

AGAINST ALL ODDS

A Story of
Faith,
Courage,
and
Never Giving Up

ANTHONY RAZZANO

WILEY

Published by John Wiley & Sons, Inc., Hoboken, New Jersey.
Published simultaneously in Canada.

For general information on our other products and services or for technical support, please contact our Customer Care Department within the United States at (800) 762-2974, outside the United States at (317) 572-3993 or fax (317) 572-4002.

Wiley also publishes its books in a variety of electronic formats. Some content that appears in print may not be available in electronic formats. For more information about Wiley products, visit our web site at www.wiley.com.

Library of Congress Cataloging-in-Publication Data:

Names: Razzano, Anthony, author.
Title: Against all odds: a story of faith, courage and never giving up / by Anthony Razzano.
Description: Hoboken, New Jersey : Wiley, 2024. | Includes index.
Identifiers: LCCN 2023014988 (print) | LCCN 2023014989 (ebook) | ISBN 9781394199716 (cloth) | ISBN 9781394199723 (adobe pdf) | ISBN 9781394199730 (epub)
Subjects: LCSH: Razzano, Anthony. | Burns and scalds in children—Patients—United States—Biography. | Accident victims—United States—Biography. | New Castle (Pa.)—Biography
Classification: LCC RD96.4 .R373 2024 (print) | LCC RD96.4 (ebook) | DDC 617.1/10083—dc23/eng/20230703
LC record available at https://lccn.loc.gov/2023014988
LC ebook record available at https://lccn.loc.gov/2023014989

Cover Design: Paul McCarthy
Cover Image: Courtesy of the Author

SKY10053065_081023

Contents

Foreword

Every once in a while, we come across stories that stop us in our tracks, causing us to reconsider our own capacities for resilience, determination, and self-belief. Anthony Razzano's *Against All Odds* is one such story that serves as a beacon of inspiration, illuminating a path of triumph over adversities and profound resilience. His journey from being a young survivor of a catastrophic fire to becoming a successful certified public accountant, NFL agent, husband, and father is not just a remarkable tale of survival but also an incredible lesson on how to thrive in life and business.

As Anthony so powerfully conveys, the challenges we face in life, whether they are life-threatening or self-imposed barriers of the mind, are not there to define us but to help us define ourselves. His remarkable recovery journey and subsequent professional success illustrate this principle profoundly. A catastrophic accident might have knocked him down, but it was his ability to rise, to keep pushing, and to refuse to be defined by his circumstances that has made him who he is today.

In *Against All Odds*, Anthony shares invaluable wisdom about resilience, self-belief, and success—wisdom that has been forged in the crucible of unimaginable hardship and struggle. Whether it is about dealing with setbacks in business or facing personal hardships, he underscores the importance of seeing past the immediate obstacle to find the opportunities that lie within. He writes, "the only failure in life was not to try." These words resonate with profound truth for anyone who has ever faced daunting odds, in business or in life.

In our professional journeys, we often encounter roadblocks and challenges. However, as Anthony's story reminds us, the mindset and tactics that we deploy to overcome these challenges can shape our successes. Anthony's life is a testament to the power of unwavering self-belief and hard work, and the story he shares in this book can serve as a powerful guide for anyone looking to succeed in business or personal life.

What particularly resonates about Anthony's journey is his relentless pursuit of knowledge and the emphasis on teamwork. Anthony reminds us that no one achieves success alone. Just as he had his team of doctors, family, and caregivers during his recovery, it's essential in business to have a dedicated team that shares your vision and contributes their unique skills and insights.

Furthermore, his story underscores the importance of continuous learning and adaptability. Regardless of the obstacle you're facing, becoming an expert in understanding it, just as Anthony did with his recovery, allows you to formulate strategies to overcome it effectively. These principles are as applicable in business as they are in life.

Perhaps the most inspiring aspect of Anthony's journey is his ceaseless optimism and unwavering faith. His belief that there is a blessing wrapped in every struggle is a powerful reminder that our perspectives can often shape our realities. This philosophy permeates every aspect of Anthony's life, from his personal recovery journey to his success in business, and it serves as a profound lesson for all readers.

Anthony's remarkable story of resilience and triumph is an inspiration to us all, but *Against All Odds* is more than just an inspiring story. It's a blueprint for success. It shows us how to harness adversity, believe in ourselves, form and work with a strong team, continuously learn and adapt, and maintain an optimistic perspective.

As you delve into this extraordinary book, I hope that you, like me, will be inspired by Anthony's story and draw strength from his example. More important, I hope you will see in his journey a road map for your own path to success, no matter what challenges you may face along the way.

Enjoy the journey. I assure you, it is an extraordinary one.

—**Scott Empringham**
CEO/founder, Empringham Media Group, LLC

1

Happy Halloween

I THOUGHT THE butterflies had died long ago, migrated south with the adventure of my youth. Today, they reappeared, and my stomach is in turmoil. Don't get me wrong, I love my life. There's plenty to be excited about. I have a beautiful wife, daughter, and son. I have a successful CPA and investment practice in Western Pennsylvania. I'm grateful that I never had to work a backbreaking, deafening manufacturing job as did so many of the men who built this town. But today, I am more nervous than I have been in years, because I'm about to coach my son Anthony in his first tackle football game at the historic Taggart Stadium.

In our hometown, New Castle, Pennsylvania, there are two religions: Sundays are for church and autumn is for football. The people of New Castle are blue-collar, hardworking people. A good portion of our town is of Italian descent. In fact, most of us can trace our roots back to the Province of Caserta, in the Campania Region, which is located off the Amalfi Coast of Italy. Local legend tells of a St. Vitus Catholic Church in Caserta, which is the reason we are members of St. Vitus Church in New Castle.

As important as our faith is, weekends in the fall belong to football. As a boy growing up in New Castle, getting your first football jersey is just as much a rite of passage as your first kiss. In most families here, the sporting tradition traces back generations to the 1920s, when the first major wave of immigrants came from Italy in search of work, often to send money back home so that the rest of the family could come over to build a new life.

Now, I'm helping my children build their lives. But today is Anthony's day; he will take his first steps carrying the Razzano family's proud football legacy to the field in his most important game to date. Coaching football doesn't make me nervous. In some ways, I feel I was born to be a coach. But this game is different. I want my son to taste the glory that not only I have known but that also has been carried on for generations in my family.

Don't believe anyone who tells you that you can't travel back in time. Feeling those butterflies at this time of year awakens my senses and memories of a time when I was 12 years old, sitting in my room, looking at my uniform and shoulder pads, getting ready for the biggest day of my life.

I remember the exact date of my first big game: Saturday, October 31, 1987, Halloween, and the weather was absolutely perfect. The smell of football was in the air. That kind of weather doesn't test your faith. You just knew that God was alive in the beauty of the crisp blue skies and the comfort of the autumn breeze. Tonight was the night that I would gaze up at the stars and step into the next phase of my life. As a Pop Warner player, I was about to play my very first night game under the lights at Taggart Stadium, one of the oldest and most hallowed football stadiums in America.

In 1929, Taggart was one of the first football fields to have lights installed for night play. In the 1940s and 1950s, more than 12,000 people would cram into the bleachers for big games. Since then, playing under the lights has been sacred in our community, a gift from God. I will never forget the anticipation; I could not wait to step on the field and add to the family football tradition.

Thinking back, I can't help but remember the four years leading up to that moment. They were tough. My older brother

Eugene, known to all of us as GeGe, and I lived with our mom. Dad was as handsome as they come and quite the ladies' man. Mom was beautiful as well.

When they met in 1968, Dad was 17, trying to thumb a ride on Mill Street. Mom, who was 20, gave him a lift and they became inseparable. A few months later, after Dad's 18th birthday, they got married, and the following year, they had GeGe. The overwhelming passion that fueled their love also fueled their fights. When those two stubborn tempers battled, the room became hotter than any steel mill in Pennsylvania. Even though they truly loved one another, and still do, the intensity of their fights grew and one night, out of the blue, after 15 years of marriage, they separated on a whim.

When they separated, Dad moved crosstown for a while. But now, he was about to move with his new girlfriend and their kids to a house just a few blocks away from us. I wouldn't have to get picked up and dropped off anymore. I could just walk to Dad's by myself. A small step toward normalcy.

Mom took a while to get over the separation. Once the traditional Italian housewife who took care of the kids, Mom went to beauty school and got a job at a local hair salon. But everyone knew she was a talented cook. So, she took a leap of faith and was working on opening a new coffee shop in downtown New Castle. In two days, Mom would be opening the doors of her business and the start of her new life. Despite the nerves of starting a business and having a payroll to meet, it was obvious how excited she was for the fresh start.

The week before my first big game, tensions were particularly high between my parents. My mother needed money, presumably for the rapidly approaching opening of the coffee shop, and she showed up at my dad's office building to get it. When he refused to give it to her, she became angry and the two fiery tempers were at it again. She screamed as loudly as she could for everyone to hear. He acted like he didn't care. That made it worse, and she swept all the papers off Dad's desk. Eventually, the police were called to escort her out of the building.

During the week, as I split time between their homes, each would make sure to let me know whose fault the incident was.

"Your dad doesn't want to pay."

"Your mom was acting like a lunatic."

The biggest changes were to the holidays. From the time I was born, our big Italian family celebrated with enormous feasts and celebrations. The feeling of love always filled the room. But now, GeGe and I would spend most of our holiday time on the road, shuttling between other relatives' homes—first Mom's family, then Dad's. Instead of being excited about the holidays, we couldn't wait for them to be over.

I used to enjoy all of us being together as a family so much. Now that I had two homes, it was as if I didn't have any. Mom had to move us to a much smaller house several blocks away, putting more distance between me and my best friends Artie and Johnny. When you're 12, it doesn't matter why. All you know is that you can't see your friends as much, and it's not cool.

By this time, although I was just 12, it felt like I was on my own. GeGe had just started his freshman year at Westminster College. Once Mom and Dad split, GeGe unwillingly became something of a guardian to me. He and his friends—Yawgie, PJ, and Zub—were as tight as you could get. They did everything together, and they allowed me to tag along. But there were no mascots in this crew. I had to keep up.

Through watching them, I learned what was cool—what music to listen to, how to dress. And I had to do everything I could to fit in. I wasn't allowed to be an ordinary kid. If I goofed around during a card game or interfered with a game of pool the way young kids do, they wouldn't tolerate it. Everything was a competition. And if we bet a few bucks on a game and I lost, I had to pay up. No discounts.

But there were benefits. Lots of them. The older girls who hung with GeGe's crew would spoil me with attention, which gave me a lot of confidence. When I was with girls my own age or even a few years older, I had the courage to ask them to take a walk with me, to ask for a kiss. I was maturing much faster than the average 12-year-old because I had to.

Now that I was in junior high, I was meeting kids from all over town. In elementary school, you were mostly with the kids closest to home. I started hanging out with older kids, and my house became one of the places to do things when no adults were home.

I was meeting everyone—the best athletes and the prettiest girls. The night before the big game, we'd gone to a Halloween party at Jessica Joseph's house, and we had a blast. The girls dressed up as football players. The boys dressed as cheerleaders.

That night, my friend Z and some other kids were playing around with a Ouija board. They conjured up two words: *Anthony* and *hurt*. It freaked everyone out, me most of all. But Ouija boards were kids' stuff now. We were onto bigger things. At the end of the night, when we were leaving the party,

I kissed every pretty girl on the cheek goodbye. I was becoming my own man. GeGe and the boys would have been proud.

When I got home, above the laundry chute in the bathroom, I found a container with Ace bandages in it. While I watched TV with my mom in the living room, I began wrapping my legs with some of the bandages. My mom asked me why I was doing it, and I couldn't give her a reason. I didn't have a reason. I was just goofing around. Sometimes, when you're acting several years above your age outside the house, when you get home, you just want to be a kid again. I didn't have to be cool once I was home.

But the next morning, I was back to acting above my age. Mom had to head over to the shop to get things ready for the opening on Monday. I was wishing I could fast-forward to get to the evening already. I wanted to put my uniform on right then and step under the lights at Taggart Stadium like the Razzano men before me. Dad played football there. So did Uncle Bob and Uncle Johnny. Uncle Rick was a legend in New Castle, and he went on to play in the Super Bowl for the Cincinnati Bengals. And Uncle Tony, who started the Razzano family football legacy, became known as a legendary NFL scout for the San Francisco 49ers who helped them decide to draft a guy named Joe Montana.

The Razzano name is synonymous with football in New Castle. So much so that the number 42 is retired. You cannot wear it unless your last name is Razzano. Tonight was going to be the first night I would wear number 42 and take my first step toward continuing the legacy. The hours left to pass until then seemed like a lifetime.

I called up my friend Todd, whom we lovingly called Dopey. He was home with his brother Brock. We hung out, wrestled around with one another for a little bit to blow off some steam, and then Todd wanted to go back in and take it easy before the night's game. So I walked to Z's house, the kid who'd been playing with the Ouija board. His parents were home, so we decided to go through the woods to get back to my house where we could hang out and be left alone.

Along the way, we ran into a few ninth graders who had been riding their quad motorbikes along the trails. They had stopped and were doing something odd. They had their faces pressed down close to the front of the seat of their bikes. When we asked them what they were doing, they told us they were huffing gasoline. When you sniff gas like they were, they said it can make you feel as if you've been drinking alcohol.

We knew who the kids were, but we didn't know them that well. They weren't bothering anyone; they had just gone into the woods, away from prying eyes, to have some fun. These were the type of kids who would listen to heavy metal, music that creeped me out, to be honest.

We kept walking over to my house because I knew we could hang out without adult supervision. When we got there, Z said he had a pack of cigarettes, but he didn't have a lighter. So, I ran in the house and grabbed a pack of matches. The match pack was black with white writing; it said Dapper Dan Appecelli, City Council. I looked on the clock of the microwave; it was now 1:53 p.m.

Z and I walked into my cinder-block garage that didn't have any cars in it. The house was so small so we used the garage to store as many things as possible. Dad kept some of his old restaurant equipment in there. He also had two huge glass jugs that we used to store the wine he would make. Just the week before, we'd cleared out a few things to make room, including a stash of fireworks from the Fourth of July. But the gas-powered lawn mower was still there, along with a metal gas can.

With nothing to do and all day to do it, Z and I had the idea to try sniffing gas ourselves. We closed the garage door for privacy from the neighbors and opened the gas tank cap at the bottom of the mower. Z lay down on the ground first and tried it. I sat on an old kitchen chair with the gallon gas can, so we were both sniffing gas. At first, I was just peeking up to see if he was really doing it. After a few minutes, he asked if we could switch spots and I agreed.

I put down the gas can I was using and laid down some newspaper because I didn't want to get my blue Gregal Construction team baseball jacket and white sweatpants dirty on the garage floor. Sniffing the fumes made me feel sleepy. I drifted in and out of consciousness. And even though I've replayed this scene over in my mind a million times, I'm not exactly sure what happened next. But when I came to, I frantically jumped to my feet, engulfed in flames! I was a ball of fire, literally! At the time, I didn't know how it started, all I knew was I had to get out of there alive.

2

On Fire!

WHEN YOU GROW up Catholic, you have this idea in your head of what hell might be like. And now, I found myself in my own personal hell, my body in flames, screaming, desperately trying to get out of the garage. A moment of sheer terror, a living nightmare.

I was captured by fire, surrounded by an inferno of sweltering heat that was eating me alive. The pain was so intense that my mind still will not allow me to relive it. I remember the crackling of the red flames as they were engulfing my clothes, consuming my life. As I fought to escape, every second changed me; I would never be the same. I couldn't have been on fire for that long. Maybe 30 seconds? A minute? But it felt like an eternity.

A few hours earlier, I was a child getting ready for a football game. Now I was fighting the most intense battle of my life. To some degree, each of us goes through a transformation at about the age of 12. Our voices change, we grow, we get stronger and more mature in so many ways. But this transformation, this moment, was impossible to imagine. It was a lesson in how fragile life can be.

My friend Z ran out of the garage through the side door, and it closed behind him. I tried following him out, but I couldn't get the door open. Trying to get some leverage, I leaned up against those huge glass jugs that my father usually had filled with homemade wine. The heat from the flames on my body was so intense, the jugs shattered.

I could hear the fire crackling as I was trying to put it out with my hands, but I couldn't escape the inferno. I cried out with a bloodcurdling scream as I fought to escape the garage.

The intensity of the heat was melting me. I knew I didn't have long; it was a panic like no other. My left hand was so hot, I put it inside my jacket pocket and the clothing immediately melted around it. I pulled it out and shook off the flames, desperately pushing on the door to open.

With my right hand on the doorknob and my left braced against the window, I pushed and pushed at the door, frantically screaming, trying to free myself. The heat from my left hand forged an imprint on the glass. The harder I pushed at the door, the less I could move it, until finally, I realized that I had to pull the door open.

Once I made it outside, the fresh air only gave the fire new life and more intensity. It was then that I saw the face of an angel. Her name was Mary. Mary Ryan was a woman older than my mom who lived two doors down from us that we didn't know too well. She was the first to see me.

Mary had heard the screaming in my garage. As I watched her making her way to our yard, I felt a strange calm come over me, like the presence of a hand on your shoulder when you can't do anything but cry. It gave me peace under fire, literally.

As loud as she could, Mary yelled, "Rooooooo-wuhlllll-llllah," finding three syllables in a one syllable word in a way that only a Western Pennsylvanian can. And so, I rolled.

Soon, another Mary appeared. Mary Hartman and her husband, Henry, lived right next door. Mary Hartman had heard my screams as well and yelled to her husband that someone was on fire outside and to come quickly.

Henry Hartman was a retired executive at Johnson Bronze, a big local factory. He ran outside and into his garage, where he grabbed an army blanket and darted toward me. With no concern for himself or his well-being, he took the blanket and covered me in it as I continued to roll myself along the ground. Once Henry got the blanket around me, the flames finally disappeared. There I was on my back lying in my yard, charred from head to toe, stunned, trying to catch my breath and process what had just happened.

Z was hysterical, squealing, yelling at me, "Don't tell anyone what happened! Don't tell!" I didn't know what he meant. I thought he was talking about us sniffing gas. I couldn't begin to think about how the fire started. But now I know that's what he was talking about. "Leave him alone," Mr. Hartman said, calmly and firmly. "Go stand in the alley."

I was breathing rapidly as I lay there in the grass, cocooned in the blanket, looking up at the crisp blue sky, once again feeling the cool autumn breeze touch my face. I didn't know what my future might hold, but I was thankful that the intensity of the fire had ceased. It was at this moment that I met the eyes of Henry Hartman.

"Are you okay?" he said as steadily as he could.

"Yeah . . .," I said. "I think I'm okay."

But I knew I wasn't. I could see the smoke still rising from underneath the blanket. I could smell the fire. I knew it was really bad. "Am I going to die?" I asked Mr. Hartman. "Oh, no. No. No. You are not going to die," he said. I believed him. After a pause, I asked Mr. Hartman the next question that came to mind. "Will I be able to play in the football game tonight?"

"Oh . . . I think we're gonna have to get you better before you can go and play football again," Mr. Hartman said.

He kept speaking to me as the Marys were talking loudly to each other. After calling 911, they were anxiously trying to figure out where to reach my parents. My mom was at the new coffee shop getting ready for the grand opening on Monday. The trouble was no one knew the number of the new shop. Before cell phones, texting, and email, delivering a message to someone in 1987 was a much greater challenge.

I was always good with numbers, so I spouted off the phone number to the coffee shop as I continued to lie there with my skin smoldering underneath the blanket. When the phone rang at the coffee shop, they must have been surprised. Who would be calling? The shop wasn't even open for business yet. They had no idea that they were about to receive a call that would change all of our lives.

The person who answered heard someone frantically yelling that a boy was burned before they hung up. At first, they thought it was probably a prank. My mother overheard the call as she stirred a big pot of wedding soup. A chill ran over her body, a certain intuition that she can't explain. Mary Ryan would then call Ricky's Hair Salon, my mother's old job, looking for her. The hair salon relayed the message to my mom that I was badly burned. In that moment, her heart began to pound as she raced to the hospital.

The neighbors also tracked down Dad, who was at his house with his girlfriend and their children. His girlfriend answered the phone and immediately handed it to him. Dad ran out the door. Before he could even gather the full story, he jumped into his car and sped to the house.

John Presjnar, the first ambulance driver to reach the house, ran across the lawn and saw me rolled up in Mr. Hartman's blanket.

When he arrived, all he could see was my face, untouched by the fire.

"Are you okay?" John asked.

"Yeah, I think I'm okay," I said.

"Do you mind if I take a look under the blanket?" he asked.

"No, go right ahead," I said.

When he looked under the blanket, all he saw was the remains of my charred clothes and third-degree burns all over my body. Imagine if you poured hot white wax on your skin. That's what it looked and felt like. My body was completely white from the third-degree burns.

"Oh, my!" John said when he looked under the blanket. Not wasting a moment, he sprinted to the ambulance to grab some IV bags. But where could he insert the IV? Unable to locate any veins on my charred arms, John inserted the IV directly into my neck. Burn victims often suffer and sometimes die from intense dehydration. Without your skin, your body can't retain any of its fluids. Had John not gotten those fluids into me right away, the burns would have killed me. They still probably should have, but somehow, Henry Hartman, two Marys, and a John gave me a chance to live.

Lying on the lawn, I imagined this is what it must have felt like to be on a battlefield. There was chaos all around. People screaming at one another. Sirens. Medics acting with a life-or-death urgency. The rest of the area seemed still except for the disorienting chaos swirling around me.

The paramedics lifted me onto a gurney, and I could hear the liquids leaving my body. As fast as the IV was putting fluid into me, the liquids were permeating my charred skin. It sounded as if someone had poured a bucket of water on the ground—a sound that will stay with me forever.

The police and fire department had arrived as well, and time was of the essence. They had to get me to the hospital. Tommy "Duck," a good friend of my father's, was a fireman. His son was my good friend. I had known Duck all my life. If you were to draw a picture of a tough man, you would draw Duck. And he always had something funny to say. But that day, he couldn't say anything. One of the toughest men I had ever known had tears in his eyes. He could barely look at me. And that was the first time I really knew how bad it was. I could see the pain on his face.

By the time my dad arrived at the house, the ambulance was already transporting me to the hospital. He looked at Duck, who stands about six-foot-five, and all Duck could do was cry. It tore my dad to shreds as he raced to the hospital, not knowing what to expect when he saw his son. The drive to Jameson Memorial Hospital is only a few minutes away, but the truth is we all lived a lifetime in those minutes. Even so, no one could be prepared for the paths our lives would take. With every potential outcome, our lives have changed forever.

3

The ER

THERE IS SOMETHING about the color white that feels pure. As I was lying in the yard, the paramedics removed the blanket Mr. Hartman used to put out the flames. They covered me with a shiny white sheet. I wasn't sure what the covering was made of, but I could tell they were terrified as soon as they saw me. The looks on their faces showed that this was a life-or-death circumstance. I can't begin to imagine how they must have felt; one moment they were drinking a coffee on a beautiful Saturday afternoon, the next moment they were called into action to rescue a young patient so badly burned that he might not make it to the hospital alive.

None of them will ever forget what they saw: 87% of my body was covered with third-degree burns. The paramedics knew they had to protect my fresh wounds from infection, while at the same time preserving my body temperature. They brought a flat wooden gurney to the ground where I lay and asked me if they could turn me on my side. They rolled me to each side, tucking the white sheet completely underneath my body. Then they lifted the sheet with me on it and put me on the gurney and placed me in the ambulance.

As the ambulance began speeding toward Jameson Memorial Hospital, every vibration came with a new, painful sensation that I had never known before. They had recently begun paving the road along Highland Avenue. The unpaved road caused the ambulance to bounce and sway as it sped toward the hospital. Every bump made the straps around my body feel like vice grips. Although most of my nerve endings were destroyed from the fire, the ones that survived were completely exposed. They were tender, open wounds that caused immense pain with the slightest vibration.

I knew the burns were bad, but for the moment, I couldn't see them. I could only feel them, especially where the straps rubbed against the wounds. When you're 12, it's hard to look too far into the future, even if the future looks dire.

Within a few minutes, we were at the hospital, which was already buzzing as the doctors and nurses awaited my arrival. To do what, they weren't sure. From what I could overhear, they wanted to get me to a burn unit as soon as possible. The doctors and nurses at the ER, well-meaning as they were, weren't prepared to see a patient like me.

I was a familiar face to the ER doctors and nurses at Jameson's. I was the kind of kid who played hard and usually brought home a medical souvenir. By that point, I had probably been in the ER about five times to receive stitches for cuts or a cast for a broken arm. But this time was different. Doctors never saw a body burned like mine unless they had worked in a war zone. And if you did see a body burned that badly, you weren't looking at a patient. You were looking at their remains. As I was being wheeled straight past triage and into the main ER, the doctors had to figure out how to keep me alive long enough to make it to a burn unit. It was almost as if you could hear the clock of my life ticking away.

I was immediately met by Dr. Carolippo and his medical team. They greeted me and gently removed the white shiny sheet from my body, folding it down and placing it on a nearby counter. I could see the sadness in Dr. Carolippo's expression, but he showed me a tender kindness I will never forget. I was completely exposed. He asked me what happened, and I told him, as best I could. He grabbed my right hand to comfort me and told me I'd be okay. He protected me in those moments from every fear or feeling of remorse and began preparing for me to travel to the burn unit at West Penn Hospital.

The last time Mom had walked into the ER was three months earlier in July, when my grandmother Rosie, my mother's mother, passed away. Grandma Rosie had suffered an unexpected heart attack at her home. By the time they rushed her to the hospital, she was with the Lord. My mother arrived at the ER shortly thereafter, holding me and GeGe's hands, and was greeted by Dr. Nancy Lamancusa, my grandmother's primary doctor. Her father owned the market on the south side of town, and we had known her for years.

That day, Dr. Lamancusa had gone out to the lobby to meet my mother, because she knew us so well. She wanted to prepare her for the reality that Grandma Rosie was no longer alive. She offered my mother a Valium to help stabilize her emotionally.

Today, with the seriousness of my injuries, Dr. Lamancusa went out to greet my mother once again.

"Janet, would you like a Valium?" she asked.

Hearing those words, my mother trembled. "How bad is it?"

"It's bad, Janet," she said. "You might not have much time, so you really need to use it wisely. This may be the last chance you get to see your son."

My mother's knees buckled. It wasn't until that moment that she realized I might not make it. In fact, Dr. Lamancusa was basically telling her to say goodbye while she had the chance. At that point, my body could have gone into shock at any moment, which could cause my heart to stop, a convulsion, or a stroke. Every minute I was kept stable and could talk was a blessing. Take the blessing, the doctor was saying. Use it wisely, or you'll regret it.

Those few moments, that act of kindness by Dr. Lamancusa, gave Mom a chance to compose herself before she came into the ER. When she did enter the room, the white shroud was gone, and I was prone and naked on the bed. The doctors and nurses wouldn't allow anything to touch me. I was literally an open wound. They didn't know where to put the blood pressure cuff, much less the stethoscope. I was burned from head to toe. Blood was seeping from my body. All they could do was continue to pump IV fluids into me, desperately trying to keep me alive as long as they could. Maybe give my dad enough time to get there as well.

Generally speaking, my mom, Janet Razzano, was a very emotional person and often impulsive in her reactions at times. But not that day. After talking to the doctor, and with what little time she had left to talk to me, she put on a brave face. She was holding it together for me.

When she saw me, she immediately greeted me with a smile. All I could manage to say was "I'm sorry," before I started to cry. The emotions that I had been able to keep in check suddenly opened up. I knew that no matter what happened, even if by some miracle I survived this, our lives were going to be changed forever. There was so much I still wanted to do. I wanted to play ball. I wanted to be a kid. But what I wanted most of all was for my mom and dad not to suffer.

I love both of my parents very much. And even though the last few years had been difficult with them being separated, we all loved each other, and I couldn't bear the thought of their pain. I know it sounds strange to hear this from a child's perspective, but I wasn't afraid of what was going to happen to me. The only thing I feared was what my father's and mother's lives would be like if I didn't survive—the overwhelming grief they would have to carry every single day. I wasn't sad for myself. I was sad for them.

My mom gently wiped the tear from my face with the back of her hand. "No, son. Don't be sorry," she said. "You're gonna be fine, sweetie. We're gonna get through this."

Shortly thereafter, my dad, having sped over from the scene, came bursting through the ER doors, wanting to see me as soon as he could, but when he did, he stopped in his tracks and turned away as fast as he could. My dad had known from the minute he saw his friend Tommy Duck that it was bad, but until he saw me in the ER, he had no idea how bad it was. He hadn't been prepped for what he was about to see the way my mom was, so he needed a minute to compose himself. When he turned back around to look at me, his poker face was firmly in place. Again, all I could manage was "I'm sorry, Dad," before I started to cry again.

"Don't be sorry," my dad said. "You're going to be fine."

I tried pulling myself together. My dad was always a source of strength for me. I lifted my left hand, which had been burned badly, and showed it to my father.

"Dad, I'm not going to lose anything, am I?" I asked.

"Son, I'm not worried about your hand," he said. "I'm worried about your life."

He walked over to the side of my bed and kissed me on the forehead. Then he put his face just an inch or two away from mine. He looked me right in the eyes.

"Son, I promise you, we will all walk out of here together. I promise you that. Will you promise me that? Because we keep our promises to each other."

"I promise, Dad."

"Then it's a deal," he said. "There's nothing that will stop us."

Moving quickly, a nurse wheeled over a cart filled with giant blocks of ice. They must have been about two feet by two feet. Her plan was to pack my body with the ice cubes to try to get the intense swelling to go down.

Dr. Carolippo interceded. He was an older diminutive gentleman, about five-foot-two and very thin. But on this day, he was a giant. No one was getting past him. He stepped in front of me and said, "No, no, no, no, no, no, no, no, no! No ice! Get the ice out! It'll kill him!" The doctor literally stood as the barrier between me and the ice, waving the nurse away. "Get it out!"

As it turned out, he was right. I would later find out that all that ice packed against me would have likely caused my body to go into shock, which would cause my organs to shut down.

After the doctor managed to chase the nurses away, it got quiet for a few moments. The chaos and the buzz surrounding me slowed down as we awaited a helicopter to transport me to Pittsburgh. They needed to keep me alive a few more minutes—long enough to get me to the helicopter. They didn't want me to die in that ER. Once I got on the chopper, I was West Penn's patient to save.

Being 12, hearing a doctor tell a nurse that she might kill me was frightening. But as far as I was concerned, I was still alive, and that's all that mattered. So, I did what most 12-year-olds would do in this situation. I turned to my dad and asked, "Can I play in the football game tonight?"

That made both my parents laugh. My mom said, "Not tonight, sweetie." And hearing that sound—their laughter mixed together—was the first time I began to feel a little joy that day. Suddenly, I wasn't scared about my parents losing me anymore. I was sad that they had to see me this way, but they were here. Both of my parents were here! We were like a family again. Before this moment, it had been years since we had spent this much time in the same room—even though I never imagined it would be under those circumstances.

But the truth is, because of the fire, in that moment, we all realized the value of time. Everything that came before this— the arguments, the fights—none of it mattered anymore. We didn't know how much time we had left together, and we were determined to make the most of it. In that moment, a genuine love was expressed that I had not felt in my family in a long time. Their coming together lifted my heart and gave me the hope that things were going to be alright. Survival was more than a promise I made to my dad. It was that feeling—my mom and dad loving me together—that made survival seem possible. That made it seem worth it. It meant everything to me.

Within a few minutes, Roddy, the helicopter flight nurse, came in. Roddy worked for Angel One, the helicopter service that was called to take me to West Penn. The pilots had the chopper running, and Roddy was there to get me and put me on the chopper. He was a total badass. He told my parents that he was going to fly me to the special burn unit at West Penn Hospital. I needed to go there immediately, so the best burn doctors in the country could work on me.

My dad, being my dad, was negotiating whether there was any way he could get on the helicopter with me. Roddy, while he was preparing me for the ride, listened intently, nodding, before he just calmly said, "Absolutely not." Truth be told, they weren't even sure I would survive the flight. The last thing Roddy needed was a hysterical parent on board. They had very good reasons for not allowing parents to ride with kids, no matter how well intentioned the parents might be.

It didn't stop my dad from following me out toward the chopper, negotiating every step of the way to no avail. Roddy loaded me into the helicopter. The rotors of the chopper were already spinning, and within seconds, Angel One ascended into the heavens with me on board for the 13-minute trip to West Penn.

Once I was strapped into the chopper, Roddy put an oxygen mask over my face. I'm not sure if there was a sedative mixed into what I was breathing, but I began to drift in and out of consciousness. You might think I would have been scared, a 12-year-old, all alone again and separated from his family, unsure of what would happen next. But honestly, I cannot remember fear. I felt a sense of relief that I was being taken care of and that I was able to spend those few moments of peace with both of my parents. I remember missing my brother GeGe, hoping I'd get the chance to see him again.

As the chopper began to take off, GeGe and Zub came speeding into the parking lot. My dad hugged and kissed him as he greeted him on the helicopter pad. Mom, Dad, and GeGe were in tears as they watched the chopper lift me into the sky, unsure if they would ever see me alive again.

4

Mobilizing

WHEN SOMEONE HAS third-degree burns over 87% of their body, national statistics say their chance of survival is 0%. Literally, 0%. People don't survive with those kinds of injuries, and this was especially true in 1987. It wasn't possible to replace such a large surface area of skin—the science was not there yet. From a medical perspective, my fate was just a matter of time. But from a spiritual perspective, faith, hope, and love carried the day.

In the hour that I had been at Jameson Memorial, the dire news about what had happened to me was spreading faster than the fire itself. It didn't matter that there was no internet, no email, or cell phones, nothing travels faster in a small town than bad news.

The beauty salon where my mother once worked was the center of town gossip. They were calling everyone they could think of. Tommy Duck, the fireman who had been on the scene and was a close friend of my dad's, was telling people the horror of what he saw. My dad's girlfriend was at her house calling every relative she could.

My dad's brother, Uncle Bob, was a defensive coordinator at Slippery Rock University. He was on the sidelines with his headphones on, coaching one of the biggest games of the season. His parents, my Grandpa John and Grandma Ida, were in the stands watching. Somehow, someone managed to call the press box at the stadium. A person came down into the stands, found my Grandpa John and told him, "You have a phone call." Grandpa John walked all the way up to the press box, where he was told what had happened. He went back down the stadium steps and walked onto the field right up to my Uncle Bob, who was in the middle of coaching the game.

"There's been a fire," he said. "Anthony's been hurt badly. It looks like he's going to die."

Uncle Bob, in the middle of this critical game for the university, tossed his headphones down, left the sidelines, took Grandpa John and Grandma Ida in his car, and began speeding toward West Penn Hospital.

After I was airlifted, for the first time in four years, my father and mother hugged and cried together. Just a few days before, they'd had a massive argument about child support. Now that argument seemed so far away. All the joyous moments—my baptism, Sunday dinners, football games—they all seemed like memories about to become distant in a moment. It was a cruel reminder that no one gets to predict the day they'll lose a loved one.

My dad and my great-uncle Pat got into a car at Jameson Memorial to try to race the helicopter to West Penn. "You're not driving," Uncle Pat told my father. He knew my dad wasn't in a state to make good decisions. Once they were in the car, Uncle Pat tried to calm my dad down, but there wasn't much to say. There were so many questions, and so few answers. So, the car became silent for the rest of the ride to West Penn. What do you say in this situation? Everyone was stunned.

My dad was trying to make sense of it all. He was getting ready to move a few blocks away from GeGe and me so he could see us more. The separation had been hard on us all. Despite it, my dad always tried to be there for us whenever he could. When I slid into third base and scraped my knee, he was the one who cleaned the wound and bandaged it. When it was too hot to wear my catcher's equipment in the Pennsylvania summer heat, he was the one who shaved my head to make me feel better, who gave me packets of honey on game day to make sure I had energy and stayed hydrated.

As all the events of the last 12 years, and especially the last four, came flooding through his mind, the thought of losing me consumed him. He knew he hadn't been with me every day, but he always tried his best. And now he began to wonder, had it been enough? Despite never missing a game, always being there when I needed a ride, had he fallen short? Would he ever get a chance to make up for it?

When I was a small child, my immediate family had been very close to the church, but when my parents separated, our religious life began to change as well. It was the 1980s in Western Pennsylvania. We were a very devout town, and Italian couples did not divorce. From a religious standpoint, I think my parents felt a great deal of remorse. And although my dad had faith in God, he wasn't as involved in the church as he had been. Now, powerless, my life hanging in the balance, my dad was praying for my life. He was searching for his faith, trying to ask God in any way if he could to spare me. These prayers were silent; it was his heart that spoke them, rather than his lips.

Over at Taggart Stadium, the Pop Warner games had started, one of which was the game I was meant to be playing in. Under normal circumstances, these games would have drawn mostly family members and close friends. Today, as word of the fire spread around, coupled with rumors that I had died, New Castle, being a family at heart, came out and crowded the stadium.

In years gone by, Razzano family members had created so many glorious memories on that field. Uncle Johnny facing off as starting quarterback against a young Joe Namath in the 1960s,

Uncle Rick playing against Tony Dorsett, and Uncle Bob, who was always tough as nails, anchoring the Canes as a middle linebacker as the 1970s came to a close. It was not uncommon to hear the Razzano name echoing through the stands at Taggart. But as our name was called this night, it was much different; our town was filled with sorrow.

An announcement was made over the stadium loudspeaker about what had happened. In reality, it wasn't necessary. The small-town grapevine had already informed everyone, many of whom were in tears at the thought that one of their sons was going to die. Later, I was told that my teammates were crying on the field, in the huddle, between plays. They could barely function, let alone play the game.

However, there's something about that stadium that is magical, and there's a strength and faith that creates character in New Castle people like no other. So, just like the many Friday nights that the New Castle faithful, wearing T-shirts reading "Razzano's Italian Army," chanted "WE ARE N.C., WE ARE N.C.," they inspired victory on that field, in the face of defeat. The miraculous heart of New Castle began to rise as many of the people in the stadium marched to St. Vitus Church, where they feverishly prayed for me.

The church was filled with parents and children. There was an impromptu rosary service attended by so many loving people, many of whom were faithful but who may not have been regular churchgoers. It was the light of prayer, sparked in darkness, that caught the ears of the Almighty.

There was one other person waiting to pray for me. When the chopper landed, I was greeted by Father Mauro, who was a priest at St. Vitus before he moved closer to the Pittsburgh area and became the priest on call at West Penn. I remember the chant of his prayers following me as the medical staff raced to get me to the burn unit, how he anointed me with Holy Oil, giving me my last rites.

Also on the landing pad was Dr. William Goldfarb, the brilliant surgeon and burn specialist at West Penn. Dr. Goldfarb had served in the military and had worked with burn patients in war zones. When President Carter sent Operation Eagle Claw into Tehran in 1980 to try to end the Iran hostage crisis, there was a crash between a helicopter and a transport aircraft that was carrying soldiers and fuel. Eight servicemen died in the resulting fire. Dr. Goldfarb was on the scene to treat the soldiers who survived. He was that respected as a burn specialist.

I was still conscious when I arrived at West Penn and managed to give Dr. Goldfarb a smile. He asked me the question that every doctor, nurse, and first responder asks you when you suffer a traumatic injury: what happened?

I tried my best to explain what had occurred. He took my right hand and told me they were going to do everything they could to help me. He assured me that I was in the right place.

I'm not sure how to adequately explain it, but meeting Dr. Goldfarb in that moment was unlike any other chance encounter of my life. He wasn't nervous; he was warmhearted, and his honesty provided glimmers of hope in the darkness of an incomprehensible reality. He said they would need to examine me to see what parts of the skin on my body were "salvageable." I'll never forget that word. *Salvageable.* I didn't really know what he meant, but I knew I was dealing with a person I could count on, and that made all of the difference. Having to mature so quickly over the last several years,

I learned how to read adults, and there was something about him that I knew I could trust.

Inside the hospital, the only family member who had arrived was my Aunt Marilyn. Her husband, Uncle John Sant, was a pilot for Rockwell International. They had moved closer to the Pittsburgh area so he'd have a shorter commute to the airport. This was also helpful now, allowing her to arrive at the hospital first. With me being 12, and my mom and dad still on their way, Aunt Marilyn was the only relative there to make any decisions.

Though the doctors hadn't examined me yet, they knew the situation was dire based on what the ER doctors from Jameson had told them. So they asked Aunt Marilyn one question: "Do you want us to try to save him or try to make him comfortable?"

Immediately, Aunt Marilyn reflected on our vacation over the past summer. She was so kind to take me with her family to Ocean City, Maryland. She treated me like a son on that trip and this moment would be no different.

Aunt Marilyn, who was there to provide support, suddenly had major decisions to make. With no one else to talk to, no one else to consult with, she said, "Please, you have to try to save him."

As this was happening, Mom and GeGe raced back home to pack a bag before heading to West Penn. As they walked into the yard, they could see the burned clothes and shoes the first responders cut off my body. My charred skin floated across the yard in the fall breeze. In the garage, they saw the giant wine jugs that had been shattered by the heat of the flames. They could see my handprint burned into the window. It must have been devastating for them to witness the residue of what had happened. They were trying to make sense of it all. The lawn mower was still intact, and they didn't see anything else ravaged by fire. Something wasn't making sense, but they didn't have time to question it. They had to get to the hospital as soon as possible.

At this point in my mother's life, she had already experienced so much loss—so much that she felt she had nothing left to lose. She had been through a very difficult separation for four long years. Although the divorce was not yet final, as a Catholic mother, the separation was a heavy burden for her to bear. Even though my dad was still alive, she felt as if she had lost her husband. Her mother had died just a few months earlier, and her father was already deceased. GeGe was off at college. So, the conversation my mother had with God was very different from my dad's. This wasn't a negotiation. She told God she didn't have anyone else.

Maybe it was that my mother had spoken to me. Maybe she'd heard the calmness in my voice. For whatever reason, despite all scientific evidence to the contrary, that day she decided I was going to live. She was going to make sure of it. So she didn't ask questions, she just packed a bag as if she would be living at West Penn for a while. This was her step of faith, an unwavering step that took courage under fire.

She tossed the bag in the trunk as she and GeGe frantically made their way to West Penn. In the car, GeGe's mind raced. He thought about how, when he was six years old and I was a baby, he would always kiss my face. He did it so much, my parents would reprimand him for it. "GeGe, stop kissing the baby," they would tell him. As we got older, GeGe tested me every day.

When I was four, I'd run across the living room, and he would throw a pillow at my feet to trip me and make me fall. Then he would howl with laughter. Or he would hold several pillows over my face and make me fight my way out. He loved me the way only a big brother could—I was his biggest pest and the person he would die for. This wasn't how it was supposed to end. He was going to watch me play ball. I was supposed to be the best man in his wedding. He was supposed to be mine. Our kids were supposed to play together like we did.

When they got to West Penn, Mom and GeGe rushed through the front door. Mom had her suitcase in hand, ready to stay as long as necessary until the day the doctors told her she could bring her son home.

Though West Penn was as prepared as a hospital could be for a patient with my burns, they were not quite as prepared for the 70-plus family members and friends who would soon arrive to see me—in their minds, hopefully before I would inevitably die from my injuries.

Nothing brings an Italian family closer together than tragedy. Italians can argue, scream, and fight—even give each other the silent treatment—but when something bad happens, all is forgotten. Everyone is present, because together we are stronger.

My visitors congregated in the hospital's many family waiting rooms, and they did the only thing they could do. They prayed. Grandma Ida, my father's mother, was the spiritual leader of the group. Many of the members of her Bible study group joined her in saying the rosary.

Grandma Ida's husband, Grandpa John, was one of the most charismatic people I've ever met. He was a World War II hero right out of central casting. Fighting in the war had taught him how to handle pressure, but little did he know that those experiences would be put to use so close to home.

Grandpa John was an elder statesman in town. He was a brilliant writer who wrote policy positions for both the chairmen of the Republican and Democratic parties in our county. He was a peacemaker, and a very influential one at that. Everyone loved Grandpa John, especially me. That day, Grandpa put his charisma to work as he befriended everyone at the nurses' station in the burn unit, trying to get any little piece of information that was being kept from my family. In addition to relaying that information, as the patriarch, he kept everyone organized as they prayed with a fervor. Grandpa John didn't want to hear voices of sorrow. He wanted to hear everyone channeling hope and faith that I would be okay. He would bounce from the conference room where my parents were, to the nurses' station, and to every waiting room.

All that was left for everyone to do was pray and wait to see if I would survive the surgical procedures. No one is promised tomorrow, but everyone was asking God to promise me just one more day.

5

The Scream Room

IF THERE WAS anything lucky about this day, it was my proximity to West Penn Hospital, which has what is arguably the best burn care unit in the world.

The burn unit opened in 1970, largely due to funding from Richard Mellon Scaife. Scaife was one of the heirs to the Mellon family who had made incredible wealth in the banking, oil, and aluminum industries. They had invested millions of dollars into the Pittsburgh area. If they had lived in a city a few hours farther away, I probably wouldn't be alive today.

The founder of the unit, Dr. Jack Gaisford, was a world-renowned burn surgeon. When he was fresh out of medical school, Dr. Gaisford became an army surgeon and found himself stationed in Japan during World War II. After the atomic bomb was dropped on Hiroshima, Dr. Gaisford and a friend stayed in a nearby town for months, treating the victims of the blast. He was the kind of man who seemed like he could do anything. He wrote books well into his 90s and had a dozen holes-in-one during his life. He was a mythical figure. Meeting him felt like meeting Walt Disney.

Dr. Gaisford mentored two surgeons who were responsible for running the burn unit at West Penn when I arrived— Dr. William Goldfarb, the doctor who met me on the helipad, and Dr. Harvey Slater. Like Dr. Goldfarb and Dr. Gaisford, Dr. Slater had several years of military experience as well. They had all treated the worst of the worst on the battlefield, so there wasn't much that was going to shock them. Dr. Goldfarb and Dr. Slater were ready for anything.

They were certainly ready for me. As soon as I arrived, they went to work. I was wheeled quickly to what was called the

45

Scream Room. It is named that because the room is completely soundproof. No one on the outside can hear what is happening in there, and I would soon discover why.

Inside, the room was filled with incredibly bright light, and everything unmistakably smelled like cinnamon. Even though I was naked on the operating table, it was incredibly hot, over 90 degrees at all times to kill any bacteria in the room. The heat was unbearable.

All I could see was people racing to do their jobs. Lots of them, covered in surgical outfits from head to toe. I couldn't see a single face; I couldn't read the doctors' eyes or see their empathy—every face was covered in goggles. Between the heat and their gear, the medical staff was doing everything they could to prevent me from encountering a strain of bacteria that could have caused a fatal infection.

The first thing they had to do was clean my body. They began the process of washing it with soap and water. They were try-ing to wash away as much of the dead skin, dirt, grass, and everything else on me as they could. But every time they touched me, I experienced a pain that felt like slow, merciless torture—torture without pause. Luckily, John, my paramedic, had started the IV PICCs, the lines they insert into your veins, before I was taken to the hospital, and I was continuously being hydrated with fluids. But now they started replenish-ing my blood as well. The team was moving fast to clean my wounds, while at the same time gathering data to develop a plan of care.

Some of them began to photograph my entire body. They pulled at me, rolled me over, and rolled me back, trying to capture images that would offer any additional information on how to treat me. Dr. Goldfarb's words, that they were trying to save "what was salvageable," kept careening around my head. They were looking for any healthy skin that they could harvest and use to replace the burned skin that covered nearly all of my body.

Those photographs were how they determined that 87% of my body was covered with third-degree burns. The only areas with undamaged skin they could potentially use were the top of my head and the tops of my feet.

As I lay on the table, the pain of my burns being scrubbed was nearly pushing me to the edge. Being on fire is beyond imaginable, but the process of cleaning the injuries was far worse. In life, there are two types of people, those who fight through adversity and those who run from it. This was but one of many moments where I would be tested. Could I sustain the pain coursing through me? Or would I just roll over and die?

I did what I was raised to do: I fought, literally. I punched. I kicked. "Get away from me!" I screamed. If I could have bitten them, I would have. I ripped the IV tubes they were using to sedate me out of the PICCs. I did everything I could to make it stop, if only for a moment. I wasn't thinking; I was responding with a fire of my own, one that can't ever be taught but can always be counted on.

There were eight members of the medical team holding my arms and legs, desperately trying to keep me still. I was twisting, turning, fighting back—they were trying to help me, but it certainly didn't feel that way. If there was a device to measure my adrenaline from the pain, the needle would have broken the meter. Had I been an older man, the energy I was expending likely would have given me a heart attack.

Finally, one of the bigger members of the staff, who was the size of a pro football player, laid his body across my chest to hold me down so they could do their work. He was a big man, nearly 250 pounds. It didn't matter. I placed my badly burned hands on him and pushed with all my might, lifting him off my body. Again, he forced his weight down on me. Blood was everywhere as they continued to scrape the charred skin from my body. It seemed to be a sign that they had removed the burned skin and reached the level where my body was still functioning.

The doctors couldn't put me under anesthesia—they had to figure out if they could intubate me, so they could put me on a ventilator. The doctors could see my external injuries clearly, but they had no idea what was going on inside my body. How damaged was my throat, my lungs? Were they so compromised that they couldn't use a tube to help me breathe or feed me? The doctors had to examine my nose hairs to get their first clue. Were the hairs singed? Were they intact? That would give them a sense of how my lungs were functioning. But first they had to calm me down.

They began by giving me a combination of morphine and Valium, five milligrams of each at a time. It wasn't until they administered 25 milligrams of morphine and 25 milligrams of Valium that they were able to settle me down. Dr. Goldfarb would later tell me that he gave me enough medicine to kill a horse. In some ways, the fact that it hadn't killed me gave him hope.

The toughest part was not being able to get anesthesia for the procedures. These cleansing procedures are required three times a day, so they are done too frequently to put you under for them. As a result, I was awake to feel everything. It was like enduring unimaginable torture. I now know that many people die from suffering the pain.

It felt like I was in there for hours, enduring a lifetime of agony in exchange for what I hoped would be a lifetime to live. The cleansing process only got worse; they literally had to skin me alive. The doctors and nurses had steel brushes that they were using to scrape the burned, now dead skin from my body. As they pressed those brushes all over my body to remove the remains of the fire, the pain became even more unbearable. The morphine they had given me seemed useless. As the steel cords pressed into my charred flesh, as though sandpaper was being used to smooth my body, it felt like they were ripping me to shreds. Once they got as far as they could with the brushes, the doctors then used scalpels to slice the next layers of skin off and go even deeper.

When they were finished, they put me in a tub filled with Betadine solution, an antiseptic liquid used to help kill the bacteria and prevent infection. To this day, I can still feel that solution burning me everywhere, like alcohol on an open wound—only my entire body was the open wound. The whole process somehow managed to take the highest level of pain imaginable to newer heights. Once I was in the tub, they began scraping endlessly again. At times, it seemed hopeless.

Then they lifted me out of the tub and placed me onto a treatment table, where they covered me with a white cream and yellow gauze before wrapping me like a mummy. The dressings covered every inch of my body, except for my face.

The doctors were now able to take a small camera, put it inside my nose, and look as far down as my lungs. Thankfully, only 10% of them was damaged. It was the first good news they had.

While the procedures were taking place, the hospital's social workers were with my mom and dad in the conference room. There, they explained what the doctors were doing in the Scream Room—though they didn't dare call it that. Over and over, my mom and dad tried to find different ways to ask, "Is he going to be okay? Will he survive the surgery?" But the social workers were trained not to give answers they might later regret. They stuck to the facts of what was happening. "The doctors will come speak to you as soon as they are done," they said.

The procedures went on for several hours. After all of it was over, Dr. Goldfarb and Dr. Slater joined my mom and dad in the conference room. In 1987, doctors didn't have fancy iPads loaded with information for easy reference. They had binders. Lots of 'em. Each of these binders were filled with studies, charts, data—anything they might need to have at their fingertips.

"Your son survived the surgery," Dr. Slater said. As soon as they heard that, my father and mother breathed huge sighs of relief. "Oh, thank God," my mother said. "Thank God he's alive!"

Realizing that my parents' mood had lifted to one of optimism, Dr. Slater recognized that he needed to bring them back down to reality.

"Let's take a look at the data," he said. "To determine the mortality rate for someone in his position, we take your son's age and add it to the percentage of his body that has been burned.

Your son has third-degree burns on 87% of his body. Well over 90% of it has been burned. When you add his 12 years of age to that, his mortality rate becomes 100%. And it's hard to tell you this, but when we see patients who have been burned this badly, it's almost better if they pass away from the fire rather than suffering and prolonging the inevitable. We are going to do everything we can to keep him alive, but the likelihood is that he's not going to survive the night. If he does, he might live three days before an infection kills him. If he makes it past three days, he might make it to three weeks. But make no mistake, an infection will kill him. We would suggest you start looking into funeral arrangements."

When my mother heard that, she started crying uncontrollably, "You can't take away my hope!" she exclaimed to Dr. Slater. "You don't know my son." Trying to console herself, she asked, "Why do you have to be so brutally honest?"

My mother is five-foot-one. Dr. Slater was six-foot-two. He stood up from the table and towered over her. As he looked down at her, he said, "I'm not trying to be cruel; this is just the reality of his injuries. If I was being brutally honest, I would tell you the truth: your son has a snowball's chance in hell of surviving." Yes, he used those words.

My mother felt those words as though she'd been hit by a sledgehammer to the heart. In spite of the pain, she stood up and pointed her finger at Dr. Slater. "You're not God!!" she exclaimed. "You have no right to talk to me that way!" she said, pointing in his face. "You don't say that about my son!" Then she fell faint with grief. As my dad saw her reaction, he leaped from his seat to catch her as she fell in his arms. Overcome with sorrow, she buried her face in his chest, crying uncontrollably.

Dr. Slater and Dr. Goldfarb turned away and left the room, still unsure of what the next step should be to keep me alive. As my mom's sobs echoed outside the room, the doctors walked toward another conference room where they would consult their medical team and continue to develop a plan of care.

Dr. Goldfarb knew that Dr. Slater was right. It said it right there in the data that filled the binders. But he had just seen a 12-year-old boy lift a nearly 250-pound man off his body. *What if there was enough fight in him to survive?* he thought. *It's not going to happen,* he decided. He knew it couldn't happen but still couldn't help but question, *what if it could?*

6

All Saints Day

WHEN I CLOSED my eyes on Halloween night, no one knew if I would ever open them again. That night seemed like an eternity for everyone waiting at the hospital, praying that I would live through the night, hoping that I would live at least one more day so they could see me alive once more.

After the stroke of midnight, it became November 1. It was not only a Sunday but also All Saints Day, one of the holiest days in the Catholic Church—the day Catholics celebrate every person that the church has canonized. Praying on this day was a tradition. But today, because I was fighting this intense battle for my life, the prayers were so much closer to home.

Before people began attending mass at the churches in town, there had been countless prayers through the night. Some of these were said by family members for whom religion was a vocation. My cousin, Sister Dolores Amabile, was a member of Mother Teresa's order, Missionaries of Charity. Mother Teresa took a special liking to Sister Dolores and would often visit with her as she carried out her work for Christ around the world. Sister Dolores placed my name on the list for prayers within the Order and they have prayed for me every day since. This included the prayers of Mother Teresa, who would later be made a saint in the Catholic Church. I'm still amazed that somewhere in the world, Mother Teresa was asking God to save me in my darkest hour.

That night, by the time I was put in a room, it began to set in for me how bad my condition was. I was placed in a bed by the window: bed 1A in Room 1—the room immediately to the left when you entered the burn unit. It was the room reserved for the patients in the worst condition. The painful hours I spent having the burned skin scraped from my body in the Scream Room was a constant reminder.

Next to me in bed 1B was George Matay, who had been admitted to the hospital on the same day. George was a student at Duquesne University who had fallen asleep in his car. I was told that an electrical problem in George's car caused it to catch fire. He was pulled out of the car while it was on fire and sustained terrible lung damage from breathing in horrific amounts of smoke.

To the eye, George looked like nothing had happened to him. George didn't have the massive burns on his body that I did. His damage was mostly internal. The doctors knew from some tests that the damage to George's lungs was significant, but they were trying to figure out how badly his lungs had been compromised.

During those overnight hours, as my parents sat by my bed, agonizing over whether I would ever open my eyes again, they talked constantly with George's parents and bonded over their shared sorrow. Just one day ago, we had all woken up on Halloween, thinking it was just another day, taking our lives for granted. You just assume the people in your life are going to be there the next day, and the day after that, until the one day you realize that you never had the chance to say goodbye.

My mother and father waited impatiently for me to wake up so they could talk to me and know that I could hear them. The first thing I remembered when I woke up was my cousin Maria rubbing my foot. Maria was the daughter of my great-uncle Pat, the man who drove my father to West Penn. Our families lived near each other and were very close. Maria was about 25 at the time with long dark hair and fair skin. When I was younger, she would babysit me frequently. I always felt a special closeness with Maria. It's fitting that she was the first person I remember waking up to.

Maria said, "Anthony, can you hear me?" as she saw my eyes begin to open. I was heavily sedated but still not intubated. My voice was raspy and to speak was painful. I could barely communicate and hardly gesture; everything was difficult. The pain was merciless. Any movement was a reminder of what had happened. Even something as simple as the vibration of a door closing shut would send a tidal wave of pain throughout my body. The only respite was perfect stillness.

When I nodded my head slightly to acknowledge that I'd heard her, Maria came to the side of my bed and kissed me on the forehead. She began to pray for me. "You're going to be okay, Anthony. I love you," she whispered. I'll never forget waking up and experiencing her gentle love and kindness.

Maria then dashed out of the room, anxious to tell everyone that I was awake. Opening my eyes gave everyone a sense of relief—today was another day. To me, November 1 was the first day of my new life, a life that would now be lived one day at a time. And if God wanted me to have it, perhaps there would be a tomorrow.

I can remember my brother GeGe coming into the room. I'm sure GeGe probably came to see me during the night while I was still unconscious, but this was the first time I got to see him. Because GeGe looked after me when my parents split up, I was even closer to him growing up than I was to Mom and Dad. GeGe showed me how to have the confidence to try anything as though I had been doing it for years. He had the same swagger that my father did.

But GeGe was also a realist. He was never someone to pretend. He called things the way he saw them, whether it rubbed people the wrong way or not. To him, I was what he had left from our immediate family. He had just gone away to college two months earlier. And in those two short months that he wasn't there to look after me, he felt as though he might lose me forever. The kid who played Wiffle Ball with him for hours in the yard. The kid who slept in his room when Mom and Dad were together and whom he'd shared a room with since they broke up. GeGe used to try to kick me out of his room every night. Today, he was glad that he never could.

If I weren't his brother, he probably wouldn't have recognized me. My 12-year-old body was bandaged like a mummy, but because I was beginning to swell, I had ballooned to the size of a man. A maintenance worker was stationed in the room with me. His sole job was to mop up the blood that leaked out from my body onto the floor.

That day, the spiritual side of my brother came out. He prayed with an intensity that I had never seen in him. He asked God to put an angel over my bed, one under my bed, and one beside my bed to watch over and protect me. As he prayed, he put his hand on me and told me he loved me. When I think back on it now, GeGe was at a crossroads in his life—he was trying to become a man, but at heart, he was still a boy. At this point, all he wanted was for his little brother to survive three days like the doctors said he might. I had made it through one. Now he wanted me to fight through the other two, the same way I did when he used to hold me down and make me fight to get up. It was almost as if he prepared me for this moment.

When GeGe left the room, there were other visitors. Only two were allowed at a time, so usually my mother would stay there with me and another person would come in. Even though my eyes were closed, I could hear their voices. My mother would say, "Look, Anthony, Ralph and Glo are here to see you." I would try to give everyone a smile, but at times it was difficult to even open my eyes.

As I lay in bed, occasionally seeing the faces of family and friends, sometimes listening to their words, I could feel a mixture of love, sadness, and pity. At times, it felt as if I was at my own wake, only I was able to hear everyone's prayers as they approached the casket. Often, I would hear things like, "You're such a good boy. You didn't deserve this." In some instances, I could tell that those words were goodbyes.

Then there were other times, when I heard voices like GeGe's, voices telling me to fight. That this wasn't the end. And those voices lifted my spirits. They made me want to return to my life again. Even though it might be different, it was still mine to live.

Every eight hours, staff members would come get me to bring me back to the Scream Room to begin the process of cleaning my wounds again. The thought of going through that same painful process troubled me. Mentally, I tried to prepare myself for what I was about to endure.

"Anthony, I want you to think about something before you go in there," my dad said before they wheeled me into the room. "This is a temporary inconvenience for a permanent improvement."

I gave him a puzzled look.

"It's a temporary inconvenience for a permanent improvement," he repeated. "I got that from a PennDOT traffic sign when they were doing road construction."

When he said that, his eyes started to smile and he gave me a grin, and I laughed. My dad always had a way of putting a smile on my face and sometimes a smile is all you need.

Putting aside the fact that my father was gleaning wisdom from a road sign, he was right. I knew I was in for a world of hurt. But each time I went into that awful room, the doctors and nurses were trying to help me get better. It was painful, but necessary and temporary. It changed the way I thought about everything that was happening to me. I needed to get better. I didn't just want to survive; I wanted to live. I wanted to play football again.

When they brought me into the Scream Room this time, there was no punching or kicking. No fighting. I cooperated. I did everything they asked me to do—even as they unwrapped the bandages around my body, removing the last layer of my skin in the process. If you've ever felt the pain of ripping off a Band-Aid, this felt like that a million times over. They had to wash my open burns with soap and water, and while it was excruciating, someone always held my hand as I tensed every muscle in my body to endure the pain.

A small sheet attached to a tray was placed over my neck, so that I could not see my body. Seeing it would have been too much to bear. They would tell me how good I was doing, trying to distract me from the gruesome reality that was taking place on the other side of the sheet as they cleaned the surface of my body. I became a different person in those moments; enduring this pain and grinding through these dressing changes made me a man, yet I was still only 12 years old. Repeating this process three times a day, it never hurt any less, but my ability to navigate the pain got better and better each time. It was a challenge that I will always remember.

When they brought me back to my room, Dr. Goldfarb came in to check on me. "How are you feeling, Anthony?" he asked, lightly grabbing my ankle. Whenever I played football, I tried to never let anyone know when I was hurting. No matter how badly I got dinged up, I had to spring to my feet and run back to the huddle to get ready for the next play. In football culture, you never show anyone your vulnerability.

So when Dr. Goldfarb asked how I was doing, I slowly raised my head off the pillow, smiled as wide as I could, and gave Dr. Goldfarb a thumbs-up. When he saw me do that, he looked stunned. "Good, Anthony. That's great!" he said.

From then on, any time a doctor or nurse came into my room to speak to me, they weren't going to see a sullen patient waiting there to die. They were going to see a smiling 12-year-old greeting them with a thumbs-up, ready for whatever might come next.

Afterwards, Dr. Goldfarb met with the rest of his medical team to decide on the next options for treating me. When the doctors told my parents the night before that sometimes it's better when a burn victim dies in a fire, what they meant was that they knew the treatment would be so painful, so unforgiving, that most people would give up so they wouldn't have to experience another moment of pain. Anything that might give them relief in that moment, they would take willingly and without regret. And the only surefire relief from the pain is death.

Even though the odds were not in my favor, the medical team planned for my survival. They had to develop a plan to cover my open wounds with skin. But, since the top of my head and feet were the only places that had "salvageable" skin, and part of the treatment involved harvesting the healthy skin from those areas, it meant that I would have to be scalped. They would take the skin in one-inch-by-one-inch segments, and then they would stretch it out, almost the way you would roll out dough, into a six-inch-by-six-inch patch that they would wrap around one of the burned areas, stapling it into my body to help facilitate skin growth.

Once that process was complete, the doctors would have to figure out what came next. The possibility of using pig skin was discussed. It was an experimental procedure that would cover my wounds in the hopes that my own skin would regenerate underneath it without being exposed to potential infections. Dr. Goldfarb pressed for the team to try cadaver skin instead. This was a process that most of the world did not even know about, let alone consider trying. There were massive risks involved. The skin is the largest organ in the human body. And the human body doesn't take well to things that are foreign to it. They were certain that my immune system would try to fight off anything it recognized as an invader—including a dead person's skin. They would have to give me drugs to help suppress that reaction from my immune system. But if they shut down my immune system, the only defense I had left to fight an infection would be gone.

"If we do it, his immune system could overreact and that may lead to death," Dr. Slater said. "How long will it take before sepsis sinks in? His heart could fail. His organs could shut down. We would be causing that."

Dr. Goldfarb knew the risks well. He was one of the best doctors in the world. In that room, where they had to balance all kinds of risks, including their own liability, he was the one who advocated for me.

"There's something about this kid," he told Dr. Slater. "He's fighting back. He's still young. He's got a stronger heart than an older person. Our job is to treat him. We don't have a lot of options, and we don't have a lot of time. His life is salvageable. But we have to act. Otherwise, all those other things can happen anyway."

After much debate, to his credit, Dr. Slater agreed that they should try. Now, they had to locate usable cadaver skin. After searching the country, the doctors found that the Shriners Hospital for Children in Boston had the cadaver skin they needed, but it would be incredibly expensive to get it to West Penn. They would need to transport it on ice via helicopter as quickly as possible. With the skin located, Dr. Goldfarb and Dr. Slater took the plan to my mother and father.

Dr. Goldfarb patiently explained the procedure to my parents, underlining all the risks that it posed. He made it abundantly clear that I might not survive. "But," he added, "I believe this is the best chance he has, slim as it may be."

There weren't many other options, and time was running out. When you're losing a football game, sometimes a Hail Mary pass is all you have left. My father was a gambling man. "Do you think it could work? Could it save him?" he asked the doctors. Once they told him, while the chances were remote, it could work, he was all in. My mother was as well. They were betting on me to overcome the risks. "Just give him a chance to live," my dad told them. Because, as long as you have a chance, no matter how small the odds are, you're still in the game.

7

The Third Day

ONCE I HAD survived those first three days, the countdown clock was reset. Now the question was whether I would survive the next three weeks. That's what the doctors kept reminding my parents whenever I seemed to make a slight improvement. Every time my mom said, "He's moving his legs better! I can see it!" she was immediately confronted with "Janet, I know what you are seeing. But it doesn't change the reality of the situation."

Never once did the doctors' words cause my mother's faith to waver. By this point, many of the people who were at the hospital initially now had to return to their jobs and lives and resign themselves to receiving updates via telephone. Monday, November 2, was the day my mother was supposed to open her new coffee shop and start her new life. Instead, this became her new life: a life-or-death waiting game.

Mom was always a very firm, direct person. She wasn't the doting type. But in the hospital, she became that. And it was bothering me. I knew it was her way of showing me her love—she wanted to cater to my needs—but what I needed was to feel normal again. Anything that would make me feel like 12-year-old Anthony, the one who was already behaving like a teenager.

My dad was getting ready to start his new life with his girlfriend as well. He was about to buy a house a few blocks away from where I lived with my mom. I'd be able to walk over anytime I wanted. That was the plan at least. But now, all of our futures were on hold.

In the meantime, my days at the hospital began to feel routine. I would lie in bed and could talk for those first few days.

However, as my breathing became labored, I was intubated, meaning a breathing tube was put down my throat and a feeding tube in my nose. In these early days, I was floating in and out of consciousness. But to this day, I can still taste the vitamins dripping down my throat through that feeding tube.

The breathing tube prevented me from speaking. I could only talk for the few minutes a day when they removed it, usually right before dressing changes. My voice was raspy at best. I was trying to learn new ways to communicate. Hand gestures, head movements—I would do anything I could to get my point across, but sometimes, no matter how hard I tried, it was to no avail.

On those first evenings, when everyone was on edge, every beep of the monitor was overanalyzed by my parents. Linda Leonard was the nurse assigned to be my personal nurse. She wasn't at the hospital when I arrived, but when she heard about my case, she asked to be assigned to me. At that time, having a nurse assigned to an individual patient was a new concept. Linda wanted to prove it could work, and she wanted to prove it with me.

She was in my room most of the day, fielding way too many questions from my parents about the monitors. Linda was patient and answered them all in stride. She was aware of my parents' marital situation and could see how hard they were working together. Ordinarily, when parents were having relationship difficulties, they would have to be separated—only one parent would be allowed in at a time to keep the tension from the room. When Linda saw that my parents were working together, she answered every question they had, even if it drove her crazy at times. Once Linda had reached her fill of questions, she simply told my parents, "I will let you know when the monitors say it's time to worry." Her calmness helped soothe my parents.

During my initial skin graft procedures, I was given sodium pentothal to put me under. One of the side effects of the drug is that it makes you very gassy. That night, after the surgery, resting in bed, now without the breathing tube, I snuck out a fart. It was not just any fart, however. It started quietly and persisted. Soon, it was the loudest fart the world has ever known. And it lasted longer than you could possibly imagine. So long, in fact, that Mom, Dad, and GeGe began freaking out and started frantically pushing the call button. I wasn't saying anything, I knew I was okay, but the longer it lasted, I couldn't hide my laughter.

When Linda came rushing in, my dad shouted, "What's happening? Is he deflating?!" In that moment, I forgot the pain and just belly laughed at my all-time greatest fart. I may have been becoming a man from everything I was going through, but I was still a kid at heart.

But such were those first few days. After all of those difficult conversations with the doctors, everyone was waiting for the first sign of a symptom that could kill me, even if it was only a case of bad gas.

But, no matter how bad it got, my dad would sit next to my bed and hold my hand while he stared deep into my eyes. He would bring his face next to mine and say, "Anthony, take my strength. Take my strength, and we will walk out of this hospital together." I'm not sure if there is any scientific evidence, but in those moments, I certainly felt stronger. Maybe it was just the bonding of a father and son. But I'm convinced there was something more.

It became a ritual; after all, Dad was a Razzano through and through. He had a level of fortitude like no one else. He was a big, strong, handsome man with confidence. If you put him in a room with the biggest stars in Hollywood, he could hold his own. He just had that presence about him. He was fearless.

Dad was a true believer in himself, and he was raising me to be that way as well. Every time we went through the ritual, every time he told me to take his strength, in my mind, I felt stronger. I believed what he said.

He wasn't the only Razzano with resilience who was inspiring me to fight. My dad's brothers had come to visit from Cincinnati. Uncle Rick and Uncle Anthony were practically twins— they were born eleven months apart. Uncle Rick was one of my heroes. He's also a New Castle hero.

While he was at New Castle High School in the 1970s, Uncle Rick led the team to a championship. As an undersized middle linebacker, he was MVP of the league. Then at Virginia Tech, he led the team in tackles all four years—still the best tackling numbers in the history of the school. After playing for the Toronto Argonauts in the Canadian Football League, coach Forrest Gregg brought him to the Cincinnati Bengals where he played for several seasons, including a trip to the Super Bowl in 1982.

It was surreal to have someone who was part of our family playing in the NFL every Sunday. For home games, we would make the five-hour drive to Cincinnati to watch him play in person. I was allowed to run around the Bengals locker room.

It was every kid's dream come true. Every summer, Uncle Rick would come back to New Castle and put on a football camp for the local kids. He would pick me up, take me to camp, and afterwards, we would go swimming together. The only person I looked up to more than him was his brother, my dad.

When Uncle Rick and Uncle Anthony walked into the room, they were shocked to see my condition. I was used to seeing that expression by now, so it didn't affect me as much as it did at first. "You're going to be fine, Anthony," they told me. "You're a tough kid. You can beat this. Keep fighting."

Uncle Rick didn't say much, but he didn't have to. What he stood for is what inspired me. He was the guy who came from our small town and made it to the Super Bowl. He was the guy the NFL didn't take right away but who kept trying until he got there. It was his relentless spirit that made him the great linebacker that he was. He was not going to stop until he had the guy with the ball wrapped up and on the ground.

As I lay in my bed, I dreamed of playing football again and was determined to make it happen. Why not me? Why couldn't I be the one who battled to get back onto the football field? That spirit was in me; I knew it. It's who I am. When you think about how many kids play football, making the NFL is the longest of long shots. Yet, Uncle Rick did it through his athleticism and sheer determination and hard work. If he could do it, I knew that somewhere in me was the strength to do it as well. I was feeding off the energy of that along with my dad's constant affirmations.

Later, GeGe's friends came to visit. Uncle Rick was one of the adults I looked up to, but GeGe and his friends had as much an influence on my life as anyone at that time—PJ, Yawgie, Zub, and Socket Head.

These guys were the life of any party they attended, and they brought the party to my room at the hospital. Their spirit energized me. PJ was an incredible athlete. He made everything look easy. Yawgie and Socket Head were both huge. Yawgie was six-foot-four and the toughest guy in town. He'd fight anybody without an ounce of fear. Socket Head wasn't much smaller at six-foot-three. This was their first year away at college, but for their four years of high school, I followed them around everywhere.

Even though they were all at different schools out of town, on weekends they would come back to New Castle and play pickup tackle football at Rose Avenue Elementary School. Whatever experiences those guys were having at college couldn't replace the friendship, the camaraderie—at times, the celebrity—they experienced in New Castle. Just being in their circle made me feel popular.

Rose Avenue had been the place to play pickup football in New Castle for decades. The older guys would always run the games. Previous generations had handed the tradition down to my dad, Uncle Rick, and Uncle Bob, and they had handed it on to the next group, who handed it to the next, until it got to GeGe and his friends.

These pickup games were based on a player's merit; you couldn't fake your way onto the field. You either earned your spot or you were a spectator. I had begged them to let me play for weeks. That fall, they relented and let me into one the games when they were short a player. But it was made clear; they weren't going to take it easy on me because I was in seventh grade.

The games were physical, and it didn't matter if I was playing against boys the size of grown men. They would match me up against the smallest guy when I was on defense. And if the ball came my way, I was expected to make a play, and it was well within the ballcarrier's rights to run me over like a freight train if the opportunity presented itself. On offense, I was always left wide open, waving my hands for a pass that would never come.

The week before Halloween, the guys met up for their weekly game and let me in. Yawgie and Socket Head were matched up on opposite teams, because they were the only two guys big enough to handle one another. I was on Zub's team and was matched up with Larry Cioffi, the youngest guy there after me. And the game commenced.

As it began to get dark, it was getting close to the end of the game. I kept running myself open to no avail. Larry knew they weren't throwing me the ball, so he helped double-team one of the older guys. As the sun went down, I ran into the end zone, getting enough separation from Larry to be wide open. Zub decided, to hell with it, and heaved the ball toward me. The ball seemed like it was in the air forever. I watched it right into my hands, bobbled it back into the air, then snatched it close to my chest as I fell on the ground. Touchdown! The game was over, and we had won.

The guys raced down the field to pick me up off the ground to celebrate. They embraced me as one of their own. It was one of the proudest moments of my life. I had proved to them that I belonged. Soon, I would be catching more passes like that. Soon . . .

Seeing the guys in my room, while they still had their swagger, it was tempered by quiet prayer. There were tears in their eyes.

I had never really seen the guys like this, more spiritual. And yet, at the same time, Yawgie was Yawgie. He was as tough as they came, and he let me know I wasn't giving up without a fight.

"You're not going to give up," he said. He wasn't asking me, he was telling me. "I can't go through this. You've got to live for me. I don't allow you to die."

It may seem funny now, an 18-year-old not giving me permission to die, but it was a powerful moment for me. It had been what I had been waiting to hear. So many well-intentioned people telling me I was going to be okay. Yawgie didn't mince words. There wasn't a false bone in his body. He really believed he could will me to stay alive. And who's to say he didn't? Hearing him inspired me to fight. Those guys were my role models, and though the six years between 12 and 18 are enormous in a boy's life, in many ways they were my peers. If Yawgie told me to fight, I was ready to fight, especially if it meant getting back onto that Rose Avenue field with them again.

8

Friday the 13th

EACH NIGHT AT West Penn, my mom and dad would spend a few minutes in the hospital's coffee shop, desperately needing a few seconds of calm. They'd be awake most of the night, praying that I would open my eyes again, looking for any small sign I might survive. Taking a breather was critical for their own well-being—at least until an emergency announcement blared from the hospital speakers.

"CODE BLUE IN BURN UNIT ROOM 1. CODE BLUE IN ROOM 1."

As soon as the words rang out in the air, their hearts dropped. They left their still-warm coffee on the table and sprinted toward my room. Code Blue are the last two words you want to hear in a hospital. It means a patient is in cardiac or respiratory arrest and their condition is so severe that they cannot be moved. If the doctors are going to save the patient, they need to go into their room to do it.

My father ran as fast as he could, and when he got to my room, he couldn't believe what he saw. There were what seemed to be at least a dozen people in masks and gowns rushing around the room, but they weren't surrounding my bed, they were surrounding George Matay, my roommate. Within moments, other hospital personnel would move my bed out of the room—partly so I wouldn't be exposed to so many people, and partly so I wouldn't be forced to think about what it would look like if I were the reason for a Code Blue.

The doctors managed to keep George alive, but he was in a vegetative state. He would be in a coma for months, his parents not knowing if he would ever wake up. The doctors were unsure if his brain would ever respond again. The young man

77

who, on the outside, looked like nothing was wrong with him, who had been sitting up talking to his parents, was still there, but in essence, the George they knew was gone.

Through it all, my parents tried consoling George's parents. But what do you say to someone who knows they are about to lose their son, if not today then maybe tomorrow? He was a young man in college with his entire life still ahead of him. The dreams you have during the first 18 years of your child's life—of watching them fall in love, get married, have children of their own, and a successful career—were all fading with his vital signs.

When my parents rushed to my room that night and saw me alone in my bed, they felt an enormous sense of relief. But it didn't take long before that relief turned to anxiety. Yes, it wasn't me who the doctors were trying to save. But it could have been. And it could be me at any moment. This hadn't really occurred to them until they saw George in his bed— what if I survived the fire but was no longer me? Maybe I would continue to live this way for years to come. Years that, for my parents, would be occupied by taking care of me, by physical stress, by mental stress, by financial stress—all without know-ing whether I would ever open my eyes again or say another word. The reality of how unpredictable the future was started to set in.

Each day at the hospital began to feel the same. The visits from the doctors and nurses. The dressing changes every eight hours. The physical therapists coming in to work with me. I still couldn't move on my own so they would come in and move parts of my body so that they wouldn't atrophy. Lying still was becoming hazardous to my health.

To combat this, my team put me in a special bed that would rotate to various angles on a timer. So if I dozed off in a horizontal position, I would likely wake up facing the wall in a bed tilted at a 90-degree angle. Or occasionally, I would find myself upside down so my head was toward the floor as if I were a vampire. Often, the noise and the rotation of the bed would wake me up, so I wasn't taken completely by surprise. But the movements and awkward positions would leave me feeling nauseous for hours at a time.

Despite the Groundhog Day feeling of being there, every day I survived allowed everyone's hopes to float a little higher. Every time I did something new, everyone would immediately raise their spirits, only to have them hosed down by the reality of the doctors and their data. The voice of Dr. Slater echoed in my mother's head: "If he's not dead in three days, he'll likely be dead in three weeks."

I remember them putting a surgical glove on my badly damaged left hand. I would flex it and show my parents. "Look," I'd say. "I can move it. It doesn't even hurt anymore." My parents were happy that I was in good spirits. I was fighting. But out of my hearing range, the doctors would tell my parents that this movement didn't really mean much in the grand scheme of my ability to survive my burns. My hand was the least of their concerns at the moment.

The doctors continued the many skin graft procedures. The process was difficult. First, my mother would shave my head. When I was as bald as could be, the doctors would then scalp the skin from my head and the tops of my feet.

These procedures took place at the fastest pace possible, allowing my head and feet to heal enough so fresh skin could be used.

When the procedure was over, my scalp hurt more than the burns did. At times, it was difficult to take, but I tried as best as I could to maintain my composure and keep giving the nurses and doctors the thumbs-up sign every chance I got.

When my head and feet healed quicker than the doctors had anticipated, it allowed them to perform skin grafts in shorter time spans than originally anticipated. To accelerate the process, they immediately sprang into action and began to use cadaver skin on me. The surgical use of cadaver skin was so new that the doctors asked my parents to sign a waiver allowing them to do it. My parents signed the waiver the second they put the pens in their hands, because we had nothing to lose. I was likely going to die without it. We had to try.

After I received my first cadaver skin transplant, I was resting in my room, accompanied by my dad and GeGe.

"You doing okay, buddy?" my dad asked.

"Yeah," I whispered. "But can you take this weighted vest off my chest? It's uncomfortable."

Dad and GeGe looked at each other.

"There's no vest on you," GeGe said. "What are you talking about?"

And he was right. There was no vest. It was the cadaver skin that had been attached to my chest to cover the exposed wounds of my burns. My new skin felt like it was weighing me down in the bed. It wasn't just my immune system that didn't recognize the cadaver skin, it was my brain as well.

The day after the cadaver skin transplant, Dr. Slater, the biggest skeptic on my medical team, came into examine the work. He was happy with the initial response to the transplant, particularly because this was a revolutionary procedure. He knew the cadaver skin would eventually fall off, hopefully replaced by my own regenerating skin. But for now, the cadaver skin would provide me with protection from possible infection. Whether it would buy my body enough time to heal remained to be seen.

But I wasn't thinking about dying. All I could think about was getting back to playing football. That Friday night, New Castle High School was competing in a playoff game, and most of the town would be there. It seemed that anyone who wasn't at the game was at West Penn visiting me. My mother's sister, Aunt Carol, was one of the people in the overflowing waiting rooms on the floor of the burn unit that the staff members patiently tolerated.

Aunt Carol is a kind woman who is always there to help when you need her. When Mom couldn't open her new coffee shop, it was Aunt Carol who went and opened the business, working in the shop every day to keep things running.

That night, my mother and father greeted every single person who'd come to visit, moving between rooms, playing host on the floor of the burn unit. But above the sound of all of the voices filling the waiting rooms, you could hear Aunt Carol raise hers, and it brought the main waiting room to a standstill.

"You people need to go home!" she exclaimed, as the jaws of all my family and friends dropped to the floor. They had never heard her speak so bluntly, let alone with her aggravation directed at them.

"If you want this boy to survive, he needs his rest," she said. "How is he supposed to rest with all you people here? And his mom and dad can't be out here entertaining you all day. They need to be taking care of him. So go home."

And with that, most of the people there packed up their things and left the hospital. Then, Aunt Carol did something I will always be grateful for. She brought a radio into my room, plugged it in, and turned the radio dial to WKST. "Anthony," she said, "listen to the game."

And for those few hours, I was no longer lying in a hospital bed. I was in Taggart Stadium for the biggest game of the year. New Castle was taking on Blackhawk for the Parkway Conference championship. I could feel the roar of the crowd—I could even smell the grass. I felt like I was sitting at the game with my friend Stephanie Pidro and my pal Dopey. On any other Friday night in the fall, we would have been there together.

I could hear the fans cheering, "We are N.C.! We are N.C.!" and in some ways, it felt like they were cheering for me. Corey Eggleston was the team's running back and defensive end, and he was all over the field that night. He ran for 102 yards on only 14 carries on offense and scored three touchdowns. As a defensive end, he was wreaking havoc on the other team's quarterback. I imagined what it would have been like to be in his position making those plays. New Castle won 25-0 that night, earning them the conference championship and a spot in the WPIAL championship game at Three Rivers Stadium. They were dominant, and it brought some joy to the town after such a difficult week.

Kenny Lebovie was the radio announcer for New Castle football, and he was a legend. During the game, he even mentioned me a few times, which was surreal. It was the first time I felt like I was connected to the outside world since I arrived at the hospital.

After the game was over, Kenny Lebovie interviewed the New Castle coach, Lindy Lauro. Hearing Coach Lauro's voice was like hearing the voice of Vince Lombardi—as a football coach he was held in the highest regard in Western Pennsylvania. One newspaper columnist described Coach Lauro as being "as tough as a bad steak." He was demanding, he was feared, and he was revered.

Lindy Lauro played for New Castle's football team in the late 1930s and early 1940s, back when players didn't wear face masks. You had to be tough, or you didn't make it onto the field. In 1951, at the age of 29, when most guys' professional football careers were over, he went to play in the NFL, becoming the oldest rookie in the history of the league.

With Coach Lauro, there was no such thing as *can't*. Just the sound of his voice inspired me. I wanted to play for him, I had to play for him, just like my Uncle Rick and so many other young men who built our town. I wasn't just fighting to survive. I wanted my chance in the ring, I wanted to play for Coach! This thought inspired me to fight to get better every day.

And, every day, things seemed to be looking up. Thus far, there were no complications from the skin graft procedures, which gave the doctors a little more optimism. But just when everything felt like it was starting to improve, bad things started to happen. My heart was beating like a drum solo. At times, it would be close to 180 beats per minute, and my blood pressure was all over the place. Then the fevers began, out of nowhere. My temperature reached 106 degrees. The doctors kept taking cultures, trying to diagnose the culprit that was sending my vital signs into dangerous territory. Eventually they figured it out.

It turned out that gangrene had developed in my left hand, the most badly damaged part of my body, the one I'd been proudly flexing for my parents the day before. The gangrene went straight to the bones in my hand, and sepsis began to set in. When your body has a serious infection, it releases chemicals into your bloodstream to fight that infection. That's the reason why sepsis is so dangerous: when those chemicals are released into your blood, they can shut down all the organs in your body. Left untreated, you'll be dead in a matter of days.

The doctors told my parents their diagnosis. My left hand needed to be amputated—there was no other option. When my mother heard that, she fainted. Literally. When she regained consciousness, they asked my parents if they wanted to talk to me. But what do you tell your son, the one who wanted to play football on the night he was badly burned? We're taking your hand? You can't play football anymore? They knew it needed to be done, but they didn't want to deliver the news.

Dr. Moye was the person who did. He was an amazing doctor, who happened to have a clubfoot that he would drag slightly when he walked into my room. He had a wonderful way of speaking to me with the calmness and seriousness of an adult balanced with the simplicity and empathy that would make a child feel comfortable.

"Anthony, the gangrene has set into your left hand," he said. "The infection is causing all of the other issues that you are having."

"But look, doc, I'm moving it better now," I said, flexing my hand again.

"Anthony, this infection is not like anything else you've had thus far. Now that it has reached your bone, there's no other way to treat it other than cutting it out. If we don't treat this fast, the infection will kill you. I'm sorry to tell you this, but we're going to have to remove your left hand."

There were a lot of things going through my head. Would I play football again? Carry on the Razzano family legacy? But with all the thoughts swirling in my brain, the loudest voice was Dad's and the words he told me in the ER of Jameson Memorial.

"Doc," I said, repeating my father's words, "I'm not worried about my hand. I'm worried about my life. Do what you need to do."

And so, on Friday the 13th, the doctors placed me in an induced coma. They needed to control my heartbeat, my breathing, and my blood pressure, which were all spiraling out of control as my body tried to fight off the infection overtaking it.

I was placed on a ventilator and a host of other machines to help regulate my bodily functions. Once I was sedated, and my vitals eased into a more acceptable range, the doctors brought me into the surgical room and amputated my left hand, the fourth surgical procedure I had undergone. I had just started dreaming of getting back on the field and no sooner, another devasting blow. My hand was gone, and so were many of my childhood dreams. I wish I could say that I was sure of myself and knew I'd be back on the field one day. But I wasn't.

The field I was on right now was no game. I was dying, my hand had just been amputated, I was scalped with no skin on my head, my body was covered with cadaver skin, I was losing blood faster than they could pump it into me, and I was in an induced coma. I was enduring torturous dressing changes every eight hours; it was too much to bear.

I could hear, but I could barely flutter my eyes. I would hear some of the hopeless conversations taking place in my room and my heart would begin to race. It showed up on the heart monitors. So much so, that Linda put a sign behind my bed telling visitors to call me by name. I was fighting for my life, but it was not in my control. The battle I was fighting was a test of endurance and every minute of my life was on borrowed time. It felt like I was at my end and that was really hard to accept. The pressure was unbearable for everyone. I would think to myself, what did I do to deserve this? Why me? But, for some reason, I just couldn't let go. Even if I only had one hand to grip life with.

9

The Roller Coaster

ONCE AGAIN, MY parents were at the one place they could find refuge, the coffee shop inside West Penn Hospital. Whenever they needed a break from the parade of medical staff, the visitors, even from staring at the walls of my room while I slept, they headed down to the coffee shop. The caffeine was their fuel for the sleepless nights, and that shop was the closest they could get to the outside world at this point. As they sat at one of the tables, embracing the opportunity to take a deep breath, the intercom sounded.

"Mr. and Mrs. Razzano, please report to the burn unit. Mr. and Mrs. Razzano, please report to the burn unit. Thank you."

Before the nurse could finish repeating the announcement, my dad and mom leaped off their chairs, left the coffee behind once again, and raced toward the burn unit. The thoughts of Georgie Matay still fresh in their minds, with each step they felt the dread of choosing the exact moment that I would die to take a break. This is what life had become at the hospital—ordinary moments frequently interrupted by information and updates that could be either sweepingly optimistic or inevitably fatal.

When they got to my room, there were no doctors or nurses surrounding my bed. Instead, they found John Cigna and Jon Burnett, who worked for a local news network.

"These gentlemen from the news wanted to interview you," the nurse said.

"You scared us," my dad said. "Next time, could you please let us know when it's not an emergency?"

89

Daily life at the hospital became exhausting for my parents. It was challenging for them to spend all day and night having a constant dialogue with doctors about what might go wrong next while trying to keep my spirits high, entertain guests, and take care of the things they needed to do outside the hospital.

My mom had been forced to step away from the new coffee shop she was supposed to open two weeks earlier. My mother's sister Aunt Betty was a huge emotional support for my mom during this time, as was her eldest sister, Aunt Peggy. They had just lost their mother a few months ago, and they had already lost their dad. But her sisters were always there for her, especially Aunt Betty.

Every day, Aunt Betty's husband, my Uncle Ray, would leave their house at 4 a.m. and drive her to West Penn from Sharpsville, Pennsylvania, about a 90-minute drive. Then he would drive back to start his shift at the steel mill at 7 a.m. Uncle Ray couldn't bear sleeping by himself, so when his shift was over, he'd make the 90-minute drive back to West Penn to pick up Aunt Betty and bring her home. And they did that every single day while I was in West Penn.

Thankfully for my mom, we had an angel looking over us in Angela Pastore. Angela was a nurse working at West Penn who was originally from New Castle. In the typical New Castle way, where everyone is family, Angela would talk to my mother every day and got to know her. Eventually, she would escort my mom up to the seventh floor of the hospital, which was under construction at the time. Some of the rooms had been finished already, and Angela took my mom up to one of them and told her to leave her things there. If she ever needed a place to rest, she could go up there and take a nap. And that became Mom's home away from home. She lived in that room for weeks. No one at the hospital said a word to her about it, and I don't think it would have mattered if they did. She wasn't going anywhere. Neither were Dad or GeGe, who had been sleeping on the couches in the waiting room.

By now, the doctors had removed my left hand, and with it the gangrene that had set in and reached the bone. As my vital signs began to stabilize, they were able to bring me out of the induced coma. It looked like the infection that was try-ing to kill me had been neutralized, at least for now. Within days, the doctors resumed the process of harvesting whatever healthy skin I had to replace the cadaver skin that had been grafted onto my body. They were racing against the clock before another infection had the chance to take hold—one that could be more difficult to stop.

The cadaver skin transplant had gone well, but that skin was meant merely as a placeholder, a way to keep infections from finding their way into my body. Once they had healthy skin to harvest from me, the plan was to remove the cadaver skin as quickly as they could and replace it with a graft of my healthy skin so that my body would recognize it and keep my immune system from attacking it.

The good news was that the previous skin grafts were working and starting to take hold. No sooner would the skin grow back on my scalp and the tops of my feet—every three days or so—than the doctors would remove it, stretch it out, and use it to replace more parts of my body that were currently covered by the cadaver skin.

But the most promising discovery took place when the doctors removed some of the cadaver skin and found that my body was regenerating skin underneath it on its own. This was very encouraging to my surgeons, which in turn gave my family more hope.

Though the grafts were holding well, they were still small, delicate patches of skin compared to the normal thickness of typical skin. Because the new layers were still so thin, blood continued to leak from my body at an alarming rate.

The average human being has between 8 and 12 pints of blood in their body at any given time. Over the course of the day, about five pints of that blood would seep through my skin grafts and bandaging and leak onto the bed and the floor. Because of that, nurses were constantly pumping blood back into my body to replace what I was losing each day.

One time, right after I had come back from having my dressings changed, one of the nurses, Trish, was setting up a blood transfusion for me. Trish was a tiny woman with a high-pitched voice and a very happy disposition. As she was hooking me up to the bag containing the blood for the transfusion, she squeezed the bag so tightly that it exploded, and the blood sprayed across the entire room. It splattered on my bandages, the bedsheets, even everyone's clothes. My room looked like the set of a Stephen King movie. Typically, we hated the sight of blood, but at this point we were numb to it. So, instead, we just laughed like it was the funniest thing we had ever seen. Who would think that we'd be laughing amidst this bloody scene in my room? But that's how tense the situation was all the time. So we embraced anything that might break the tension, at least until they informed me that I had to go back and have my dressings changed all over again. That was brutal.

Because I needed so much blood, my New Castle family was called on—and they rose to the occasion. Everyone got involved in blood drives around town—family members, friends, families of friends; it seemed like the whole town was donating blood for me. In the three weeks alone, they had raised over 300 units of blood, and, given how quickly I was losing blood each day, I probably used every drop of it.

The longer I survived, the more I attracted the attention of the news media. If the presence of the television anchors in my room was any indication, I had suddenly become a "human interest" story.

The story started to find a national audience. The *Weekly Reader* was a magazine that was distributed to many schools around the country. When they heard about me, they began publishing updates on my condition. Before I knew it, cards started to pour into West Penn from kids all over the country. Some teachers even gave their classes assignments to write and send me a card. There were thousands of them—so many, it would have taken forever to read them all, and believe me, my mother tried. Some of the cards arrived individually, occasionally from kids I knew or their siblings. Other times, the cards would come in bundles from classrooms around the country.

Mom would sit next to the bed, open them up, show me the card, and then read it to me. Some of them had silly seventh-grade jokes to try to cheer me up. Others had very thoughtful heartfelt messages written in them. Just the thought of all of these kids taking the time to write me lifted my spirits. It gave me yet another reason to fight to live. This was the outside world I longed to return to and inhabit, to laugh and joke with kids my age. My mother started taping the cards to the wall of my room, and it wasn't long before the walls were completely covered with the cards.

I also received several letters from extended family members around the country. My cousin Eugene Ranieri lived in Chicago, and he was a devout Christian. I'll never forget his letter because he said that he had been praying and that he already knew I was going to survive. He included a pink handkerchief that was anointed with a special oil that he asked my father to put over my body.

My Uncle Tony, who was one of the player personnel executives for the San Francisco 49ers, brought me an official NFL football with messages written by players on that legendary team—Joe Montana, the Hall of Fame quarterback; Roger Craig; Jerry Rice. Many of the players I idolized wrote individual messages to me. No matter how sick I was, I was still in awe that these guys even knew who I was.

But perhaps the most prized possession in my room was a huge photo of a white Bengal tiger that my Uncle Rick had given me. Part of the symbolism was that Uncle Rick had played for the Cincinnati Bengals. But the bigger message was that the white Bengal was a rare species. It was his way of telling me that I was a rare breed and that I could defeat the odds.

After the news reporters interviewed my parents, they asked if they could borrow the photo of the white Bengal for their news feature. They promised they would return it as soon as possible. I'm still waiting for its return.

Maybe the news coverage started to happen because everyone was beginning to feel a little more optimistic about my survival. There aren't many feel-good stories coming out of the burn unit of a hospital. And as we got closer to the end of my third week at West Penn, the date my doctors felt it was unlikely I would live to see, things seemed to stabilize again.

But maybe people got optimistic a little too soon, because things became bleak very quickly. I had only been out of the induced coma for a few days, and things appeared to be settling down, when my vital signs suddenly were all over the place again. My body was fighting another infection. My heart rate was 189 beats per minute for almost three days straight. If I didn't have the young strong heart of a 12-year-old, that alone would have likely proved fatal. My blood pressure dropped all the way to 49/20. My fever spiked to 106 degrees as my body tried to burn the infection out of me.

Desperately trying to get things under control, the doctors gave me the most powerful antibiotics they possibly could. Dr. Goldfarb referred to it as "the Gold Standard" of medicine. When that didn't work, they decided to put me into another induced coma, my second in a week—anything to slow my heart rate, get my vitals under control, and buy them more time to figure out what to do next. But putting me back into a coma was no magical elixir. The sad truth is that once they put you on a ventilator, the longer you are on it, the less likely you are to come off it alive.

This time, the doctors didn't have an answer. There wasn't another part of my body that they could remove and take the infection with it. The drugs were proving to be ineffective. My mom and dad were pleading with them for answers—any solution to this latest and most dangerous problem, but there wasn't anything left to say. They had run out of treatment options.

As my body began another downward spiral, friends and family raced back to West Penn, the finality of that 21st day in the hospital rapidly approaching. My Uncle Bob was praying so feverishly, he was practically speaking in tongues as he tried to cast the spirit of death away from me. I was administered the last rites for the third time since the accident. Everyone was getting ready to say their goodbyes.

10

Last Rites

As THE DOCTORS feared would someday happen, sepsis had set into my body. The infection was no longer in a localized place that they could home in on and treat. It was now coursing through my bloodstream. The mobility of the sepsis in my body caused my immune system to attack anything and everything it could to get rid of the bacterial infection, including all my major organs.

Once the doctors told my parents they were halting treatment and beginning to make me "comfortable," the mood at the hospital became grim. Some of the best burn doctors the world has ever known, men who had treated burn victims in time of combat, no longer had any solutions to offer. My body was fighting too many wars on too many different fronts.

Under normal circumstances, the sepsis alone could be enough to prove fatal. But unbeknownst to the doctors at the time, my body was also fighting against hepatitis, which I had contracted during one of the numerous blood transfusions I was receiving. At that time, hospitals did not screen donated blood for hepatitis. It wouldn't become common practice until four years later in 1991. The hepatitis C was attacking my liver, giving my immune system another invader to ward off in addition to the cadaver skin, which it easily recognized as not being my own.

All these infections kept raising my body temperature as my body attempted to kill the infections with heat. But if my temperature stayed too high for too long, I would be at risk for permanent brain damage or even death. The powerful antibiotics the doctors had given me to conquer the infection weren't enough. When that became apparent to them, that's when they told my parents there was nothing left for them to do. They had exhausted every available option. They again suggested it was time to consider preparing my funeral arrange-ments. With my heart rate racing for days and my 106-degree fever, I wasn't going to make it through the night.

It was the evening of November 21, three weeks from the night I was brought into West Penn. Those three weeks seemed like a lifetime—all the surgical procedures, the scraping of my skin, the bandaging, the tubes, respirators, and blood transfusions. And now, Dr. Slater's words echoed in their minds: "If he sur-vives three days, he's not going to survive three weeks." That three-week finish line seemed like it was minutes away. And now, my parents saw it disappearing into the distance.

The doctors stopped my treatment and administered Pavulon, a drug so potent it can essentially put you in a coma. Then, everyone waited for me to die. Mom, Dad, and Aunt Betty kept packing ice against my neck, wrists, and feet, never giving up on trying to get my fever to come down.

Mom continued to pray for me, but her prayers began to shift. As much as she wanted me to live, she wasn't sure how much more of this I could take. She was beginning to understand why Dr. Slater said that sometimes it's better when a burn vic-tim dies because it saves them from suffering. So rather than praying for my survival, which she began to feel was her selfish want, she prayed for God's will. If I were to survive, she asked that I recover fully. If I were to die, she asked that I would pass peacefully.

Those three weeks that we spent at West Penn together—Mom, Dad, GeGe, and I—had a profound effect on all of us. Regardless of what had happened the previous four years, my parents came together for me, and we were a family again. Had that not happened, I probably would have died the very first night as the doctors predicted. But being together filled my heart so much, it was hard not to want more of it, even if it were just for one more day.

As word began to spread of my imminent demise, family and friends began rushing to West Penn. They overwhelmed the waiting rooms as they were prepared to pay their last respects. Grandpa John and Grandma Ida led their bible study group in prayer for me. And at this point, Father Mauro, the priest we knew well from his days at St. Vitus in New Castle, was there to administer last rites one more time. The scene resembled my first day at West Penn, when doctors doubted I'd survive that night. Together, they would hold a vigil for me throughout the night.

On this night, Father Mauro brought an unusual guest with him. She was a small, older Italian woman. My family did not know who she was, and to this day, I don't know her name. She brought with her a special oil that she used to anoint me by rubbing it on my forehead and my body. Where had the oil come from? I still don't know. Did it come from Italy or the Holy Land? Was it from a weeping Virgin Mary statue? Like her identity, it remains a mystery to me.

The older woman sat at the foot of my bed and prayed for hours. As I lay unconscious in an induced coma, her prayers were steady and confident and served as a soundtrack to everyone in the room who was enduring this experience with me.

Through it all, my heart was still racing at over 180 beats per minute. Doctors described my heart to my parents as if it were a marathon runner. It was young and healthy, so it could run at that pace for a while. But at some point, the runner tires out and eventually gives up. Hearts aren't built to beat at this

speed for more than 72 hours. They weren't sure where the finish line was, but it was in sight now.

The fatigue and stress in the room were almost too much to
bear for my family. It is one thing to experience death in your
family. It's another to be present, waiting for it to happen.
After several hours of this unbearable tension, the older Italian woman finished her prayers for me. She immediately stood
up and hugged both of my parents.

"Your son is going to be okay," she said. "He is healed." Her
words echoed what my cousin Eugene had said in his letter
with equal certainty. It was the last test of my parents' faith.
They had the doctors, the men of science, telling them that
it was over. And then you had people of faith like my cousin
Eugene and this mystery woman, claiming that it was indeed
over, and I was already healed. As much faith as my family
had, the argument for science seemed to be collecting overwhelming evidence.

As the night wore on and my condition remained stable in its
instability, the exhaustion became overwhelming. One by one,
people began to fall asleep, both in my room and in the waiting room. Eventually everyone resolved themselves to the idea
that whatever happened next was in God's hands.

In recent years, my dad had not attended church as often,
especially after he split with Mom. He still considered himself
a spiritual person, but the rituals of Sunday mass had become
less a part of his life. But over the past weeks, when it was late
at night, and there wasn't much to be done by my bedside, my
dad would go down to the hospital chapel, sit by himself, and
silently pray.

My father wasn't afraid to take a gamble. But his son was the one thing he was afraid to lose. So he was leaving nothing to chance. Every night, he would sit alone in the chapel and ask God for strength—not just the strength to get through this ordeal, but strength that he could pass on to me. My dad wanted to give me everything he had. And when he had given it all, and it seemed it still might not be enough, he asked God for more.

On this night, Dad went down to the chapel to ask for strength once again, maybe for the last time. It felt as if everyone had exhausted all of their options—the doctors, the people praying for me. All that was left was for my heart to stop beating.

As the sun rose, people began to wake again. Once they reoriented themselves to their surroundings, they looked at my monitors and still saw them flashing and beeping and pinging. Somehow, I was still alive.

When the doctors came into the room, they were also surprised that I had somehow managed to survive the darkness, but it was the information on my monitors that they found most miraculous. My heartbeat began to slow down again. My fever, once 106 degrees, began to break. Not only was I still alive, but I also wasn't in imminent danger anymore.

Was it everyone's prayers? Did my body survive the fever long enough for it to destroy whatever infection was inside of me? Was it that my heart had enough beats in it to get me through it all? The doctors had theories but no surefire explanations. To them, it didn't even matter. Once they realized that I had survived the worst of it and my vital signs were stabilizing, they immediately reverted to treatment mode and began preparing for the next skin graft operation in a few days.

By now, they had managed to remove much of the cadaver skin and replaced it with the healthy skin they had harvested from my scalp and feet. My body was covered in staples from all of the previous grafts. This new graft would continue to replace areas still covered by the cadaver skin.

After I survived that weekend, something undeniably shifted in everyone's attitude. By no means was I out of the woods; I still had a major risk of developing another infection. There was also no guarantee that the numerous skin grafts would be successful. But for the first time, everyone collectively started to allow themselves to dream that I could walk out of the hospital after all. I made it through the first day. Then I lived past the three days the doctors originally gave me. I even survived the three weeks that they surmised were the outer limits of what life I had left. My parents always had faith, but now science was starting to catch up. The doctors were beginning to feel slightly hopeful.

A few days later, the doctors gave me my next skin graft operation, just before Thanksgiving. I never thought my scalp and feet could grow so much skin, and yet, every few days, there seemed to be a new supply.

The following day was Thanksgiving, and my extended family all gathered at my grandparents' house for the holiday. Thanksgiving was one of our favorite days of the year, because it always had the three Fs—food, football, and family.

As Grandma Ida prepared the turkey, along with her famous Italian delicacies, our seats at the table were glaringly empty this year. Mom, Dad, and GeGe refused to leave West Penn, but with the attention we were receiving from the local news, a

…

restaurant across the street from the hospital named Santucci's invited my family to a special Thanksgiving dinner with all of the trimmings. Given the circumstance, it may not have been the best way to celebrate Thanksgiving, but to this day my family reflects on the acts of kindness by the Santucci family. It was a bright spot in a very dark time in our lives.

After I survived that harrowing night in the hospital, we had so much to be thankful for: I was alive. So many cards were coming in with generous donations and heartfelt messages. My parents would receive cards from strangers that would touch their hearts. It was the most modest gestures that touched them so deeply. Although we had gone through so much, we were filled with gratitude.

Later that evening, family members started to show up with leftovers from the day's celebration. Grandma Ida's home-made antipasti made the trip to the hospital. So did some of her stuffed shells. Mom and Dad rearranged the waiting room to make a little buffet for everyone. An exhausted staff was thankful that there was even some food prepared for them as well. Food is love in our family, and it was a small way for my family to say thanks for everything they were doing for us.

Though the doctors made it clear that the next fatal infection could be just around an unseen corner, that night everyone took a deep breath and relaxed. It was a holiday from everything, including from worrying. And if only for a day, we allowed ourselves to feel like we were at home in West Penn as a family.

11

Dawn

AFTER THANKSGIVING, THINGS quieted down, and we settled into a new normal at the hospital. The surgical procedures to harvest the good skin from my scalp and feet were still painful, but they had started to feel routine. By now, I had been through 10 surgeries, and no matter how many times you go through it or how skilled the doctors are, there is no such thing as a routine surgery. Every time they wheeled me to the operating room, I could see the looks on my parents' faces as they held my hands down the corridor. Would I make it through one more operation?

Each time I survived, it boosted my parents' hopes a little more. The layers of skin on my body were still extremely thin but they managed to cover me, lowering my chances of getting an infection. And though I was still losing quite a bit of blood every day, my vital signs were stable. The skin grafts were holding well. Everyone was allowing themselves to feel a little optimistic.

On December 4, I had my next major skin graft procedure. This one used the harvested skin to cover the remaining parts of my body still protected by cadaver skin. After each of these procedures, it would take approximately four days for the doctors to determine whether the graft would hold, and the procedure could be considered a success.

On December 8, Dr. Goldfarb stopped in to examine me and talk to my parents. Despite my parents' growing confidence that I would survive, I was still connected to a respirator. I remained heavily sedated. I hadn't eaten any real food in over a month. "Anthony is doing well," Dr. Goldfarb told my parents, "but we're going to need all the prayers we can get that this last graft takes." It was Goldfarb's way of saying that they've done as much as they could through surgery. It was my body's turn to do the work and heal. So, with the grafting nearly complete, a little prayer to speed up the healing was what the doctor ordered.

Four days later, the doctors felt I had improved enough to take me off the respirator. Without the tubes in my nose and throat, I could finally communicate the way I wanted. I didn't have to give a smile or a thumbs-up anymore. I could tell people exactly how I felt. And to my family, I was Anthony again— the Anthony who could speak and crack a joke.

The mood shifted dramatically at the hospital. All weekend, my family took turns coming into the room to talk to me— Mom, Dad, GeGe. But one of the people I was most excited to see was my cousin Kristen. She and her brother Jeff were twins a year older than me. Whenever our families would get together, after supper, Kristen, Jeff, and I would go off to another part of the house to hang out while the adults stayed in the living room and talked. We were very close because they were two of the coolest people I knew.

Jeff still felt a little nervous about coming into the room, so he stayed in the waiting area with the rest of my family. But Kristen was excited to talk to me, and I was happy she was there. Because it was lunchtime, she brought herself a big Italian sandwich from Angelo's, the restaurant across the street from the hospital. Pittsburgh is famous for its sandwiches, and Angelo's sandwiches were no exception.

Kristen and I talked and laughed as she had her lunch in my room. But I was so hungry. I missed food so much, I couldn't stop thinking about that sandwich.

"Let me have some," I asked her.

"I don't know if I'm allowed to give you any," she said. And she was right. I hadn't eaten any solid food in six weeks. Usually, the nurses start you off slow with soft foods like apple sauce and pudding. Maybe some soup. But that Italian sub was calling my name.

"Just let me have a bite, please?" I asked.

And my cousin, cool as she was, held the sandwich up to my mouth. I couldn't even hold it myself at this point. And while no one was around, I took a bite out of that sandwich. And to this day, it was the best sandwich I ever tasted. And then she held her can of soda to my mouth, and I took a sip, and for a moment, I was in the outside world again on a Saturday afternoon, savoring the taste of the bread and the sliced meats, feeling the sugar of the pop awaken my senses. It felt like home. I started to feel like myself again.

When Dr. Goldfarb came by, he looked under my dressings to see how the procedures were healing. He would often use baseball analogies to explain things to my parents. When I survived the first night at the hospital, he told them, "We're not even out of the first inning yet." After the cadaver skin transplant, he said, "He hasn't even reached second base." But after today's examination, he looked at my parents and said, "He's standing on third base." It was the highest level of optimism that the medical staff had shown to date. The idea of getting out of the hospital and making it home wasn't as far-fetched as it had sounded a few weeks earlier.

The following day, Monday, December 14, Dr. Slater joined Dr. Goldfarb for his rounds. He removed my bandages and looked at the skin on my chest. I'll never forget that moment. He just kept saying over and over, "Incredible! Just incredible! Incredible!" For someone as stoic as Dr. Slater, it was as if he was jumping in the air and clicking his heels.

As much as my parents had tried to temper their enthusiasm, it was hard to hide it now. My mother had started keeping a calendar of the things that happened while I was in the hospital. In November, there were stickers to mark every day that I had survived. But in December, she began to write down every good thing the doctors told us, and it started to fill up each day.

That day was the first day they moved me out of the critical rooms in the burn unit to Room 4, a space for patients with less severe injuries. Though it was only a few feet away, it seemed miles away from those first days in Room 1, when my parents never knew if the next intercom message they heard meant I was dying.

After moving into that room, I had an unexpected guest. Yuji Okumoto had just starred as Chozen Toguchi, the nemesis to Ralph Macchio's character in *Karate Kid II*. He had already been in other big Hollywood movies like *Real Genius* and *Better Off Dead*. It felt like I was living in a dream, and the dream was my own movie and I was the star. And here was this famous person whom I only knew from the movies costarring with me.

John Stallworth, the Hall of Fame wide receiver for the Pittsburgh Steelers, also came to visit me several days later. These were no longer people coming via the NFL connections from my Uncle Tony with the San Francisco 49ers or my Uncle Rick with the Cincinnati Bengals. These were people who had heard about my story and decided to come on their own to visit me. Having famous people like this come to see me made me realize how much people cared and wanted me to get better. That kindness from others was an inspiration to me.

Because it was looking like I was going to survive, I became even more of a national story. I was beginning to get more media attention with each passing week. There was one other significant milestone that day that I will never forget. I had finally started eating real food, and now I had to go to the bathroom. Badly.

"You have to get me into the toilet," I demanded. "I'm not going in this bedpan."

After the medical staff members talked it over, they devised a plan. They were going to lift me off the bed, sheet and all, and place me on a blue chair in the room. Then they would wheel the chair over to the bathroom. And then, hopefully, I could make the few steps to the toilet.

Whether or not I could walk was still unknown. The only movement my body had experienced for the last six weeks was thanks to the physical and occupational therapists who would visit my room. They would help me try to bend my knees and ankles and straighten my feet. It was incredibly painful, and it would often break some of the adhesions in my skin, but it was necessary to keep my muscles from weakening worse than they already had.

The staff members lifted me with the sheet and got me into the chair according to plan. But when I had to move from the chair to the toilet, I realized this would be much harder than I envisioned. I had not used my body in six weeks. The toilet, even by a 12-year-old's standards, was perilously low to the ground. My mom and dad held me by the arms, and as I sank toward the seat, the adhesions in my grafts began to pop even worse than they had during physical therapy. Blood was everywhere. In some ways, it was a victory. I had made it out of bed, something most people never thought would happen. But it was also a reminder of how far I had to go before I reached any semblance of normalcy.

After I finished on the toilet, I pulled my gown back on. Unable to bend my legs, I walked straight-legged like Frankenstein out of the bathroom. I exited the bathroom and walked past the mirror and sink in my room. As I dragged my IV and the tubes connected to me, blood trailing behind me with every small, stiff-legged step I took, I wondered who it was that I saw in the mirror because it didn't look like me.

For a 12-year-old, I was tall and strong, weighing over 100 pounds. I was a good athlete and enjoyed some popularity at school. But when I glanced in the mirror, I saw someone who was three inches taller, 15 pounds lighter, gaunt, and ghostly white. Blond peach fuzz replaced my dark hair due to all the medications I had been given. As I saw my reflection for the first time, I began to cry. Reality had set in. I wasn't that boy who was getting ready to play football on Halloween. I was a different kid who could barely take a few steps on his own. I was devastated.

The milestones were beginning to pile up, but in my mind they weren't happening fast enough. I no longer needed an oxygen tube. I began to eat solid food (officially at least) for the first time when I had pancakes and sausage. I started to stand on my feet and take a couple of steps with my parents' support.

On December 17, they let me try to walk outside the room for the first time. My physical therapists were happy to see me take a few unassisted steps. But I didn't want to be graded on a curve. I didn't want to be limited by my circumstance. So, as my parents held my arms, I tried to run, while my stiff legs shuffled slowly across the hospital hallway floor—again, leaving a trail of blood behind me. I still couldn't bend my knees, but I didn't care. I was going to try. To think back on the puddles of blood that dripped off my body with each step is surreal. Every step was so painful, but the pain was nothing compared to the joy of being out of that bed.

Dr. Goldfarb said that if everything continued to go smoothly, I might be able to go home in January. So, when Christmas Eve rolled around, my parents were in a celebratory mood and decided to throw a party on the floor of the burn unit.

Christmas Eve was the night that my parents would traditionally host our extended family, and they were not going to miss the opportunity to celebrate on this occasion. Together they had more food than anyone could possibly eat brought into the hospital. The wine was flowing as everyone celebrated with the Feast of the Seven Fishes, the traditional pre-Christmas dinner celebration in Italian Catholic homes. Trays of food were everywhere—shrimp cocktail, mussels, clams, you name it—and you could smell it through the hospital.

The next day, Christmas morning, my parents surprised me with my first Nintendo. I had never had a Nintendo before. It was *the* game system to have at the time. They hooked it up to the television in my room, and within minutes GeGe and I were playing Super Mario Bros. It didn't take me long to figure out how to use the controller with just my right hand: index finger on the movement button, ring finger on the speed button, and pinky to jump. I loved every minute of it.

Later that morning, a crew from *Good Morning America* showed up. They wanted to give me Christmas presents and film it. I begged the hospital staff members and my parents to send them away, and they did. I didn't want to be on TV on Christmas. I didn't want to be the disabled kid whom everyone pitied. Everyone thought that my survival was a miracle and wanted to celebrate it, and it was. But I wasn't ready to celebrate yet. My legs were so stiff, I couldn't walk on my own. I had to be held up to take a simple step. When I was able to get out of bed, the trail of blood I left behind made it look like a crime scene. And the pain and swelling from my amputated left hand was so severe, it consumed every waking moment of my life. It was becoming clearer that the marathon I needed to run to be the person I was meant to be would be far more grueling than the mile I had just run to avoid death. I wanted to get back to the life I had—school, friends, playing ball. In that bed on Christmas morning, I was thankful for everything I had overcome, but I realized that I wasn't crossing the finish line; the race had only begun. I had survived, but now I wanted to live.

12

Merry Christmas

ON CHRISTMAS MORNING, I could hear a buzzing outside my room that didn't sound like any of the seemingly endless number of machines that had been connected to me over the last two months. The buzzing turned out to be a blue remote-controlled car that Dr. Goldfarb was guiding toward my room. He had bought it for me as a Christmas present.

That morning, Dr. Goldfarb spent more time in my room than ever before, smiling and talking to my family. The fact that I had finally "rounded third" gave everyone a great sense of relief, including the doctors. Then Dr. Goldfarb gave me the gift I really wanted more than anything else.

"Anthony, do you want to go home?" he asked.

My eyes opened as wide as they could.

"YES!" I screamed with my raspy voice. I thought he meant we could leave right away.

"Let's go!" I told my parents, as I tried to climb out of my chair.

"Not so fast, Anthony," Dr. Goldfarb said. "There are a few things you will need to do first. They are going to require a lot of work on your part. We need to make sure that when you get home, you can do all the things you need to do. So, in the next few days, we will practice the things you do in everyday life—walking, getting dressed, climbing a flight of stairs. These things will not be easy. At times, they will be very painful. But if you work at them, if you show us you can do them, we will be able to release you from the hospital."

Prior to this moment, there wasn't much long-term talk of survival, let alone any real discussion of me going home. But

Dr. Goldfarb, being the maverick that he was, decided to deliver the news as a Christmas present. He felt that if I could demonstrate that I could handle all the activities he mentioned, I might be able to leave on New Year's Day. Even then, I'd be making a stop at a rehabilitation center first, where they would intensify my therapy sessions to get me back on my feet faster.

A few days after Christmas, I really wanted to see my friends Artie and Johnny. They had been my closest friends for most of my young life, and I knew they were pulling for me every day I was in the hospital. Their parents brought them to see me. When they got there, my dad pulled them aside before they entered the room and prepared them.

"Boys," he said. "Anthony is going to look very different. He's going to sound very different. He's not going to look like he did when you last saw him. But it's very important that when you go into the room and see him, you don't react to what you see. You need to treat him as if he looked exactly like he did before the accident."

But when Artie and Johnny walked in, they took one look at me, and they immediately started to cry. They tried their best to hold it together for me, but once they were in the room, their emotions spilled out. I ended up consoling them. I told them I was going to be okay, that I'd be getting out of there soon. There's nothing quite like your childhood friends, and once they got past the initial shock, we did what friends do—we played Nintendo in my room for hours. It was beautiful. This is what I wanted. I wanted to go back home and do this. I still appreciate that moment because it inspired me to work harder to get where I needed to be.

While I was motivated to get out of the burn unit by any means necessary, there were still some obstacles. As it would turn out, New Year's Day would be too soon to find a space at a rehab center. The red tape of finding a suitable rehab center with an open bed took far longer than even the hospital expected, so I had to stay in West Penn until they could find me a room at a place they felt would work for me.

Also, because my skin was still growing back so rapidly, it would easily adhere to itself, which meant I had to sleep in some very awkward positions to keep my limbs from touching each other. Rather than lying in bed with my arms beside me in a comfortable position, I slept with each arm out at a ninety-degree angle to prevent them from getting stuck to my body.

Trying to break up scar tissue and release adhesions became a daily ritual in pain. My therapists would stretch my shoulders as they rubbed Lanolin into them to loosen them up. Every time my body broke an adhesion, it felt as if I was being cut open. Blood would constantly seep out as the scar tissue ripped apart. At times the pain would be so intense that I couldn't hold back the tears. I always tried to stay tough, but I vividly remember times that my mom would hold my hand and kiss my face as I trembled in tears to get through the pain. Sometimes in life you have to have tough love to get through difficult moments, and other times a tender heart can help you through. In physical therapy, my mom would show me tenderness and love when she saw me struggling and it was very effective.

As I was learning to walk on my own, I would get overcome with vertigo. My body wasn't used to being upright, and I would feel nauseous immediately. But my parents and GeGe would take turns helping me to keep my balance. They were walking with me, encouraging me with every step. It really was a group effort—my mom was on one arm, my dad or brother on the other, while someone would push the IV cart behind me. Each step came with grimacing pain, but it also embedded in my brain how fortunate I was to have my family supporting me through every obstacle. Although I was 12, it was as if I was a toddler learning to walk for the first time.

As the days went on, I made progress. Eventually my physical therapist challenged me to walk to the therapy room each day, rather than riding in a wheelchair. I still had to be lifted out of bed into a chair, then my family would help me to my feet. With my head spinning, my stomach in my throat, and my knees unable to bend, I would take one small Frankenstein step at a time, gingerly inching myself forward. At first, I could barely make it through a hallway or two. But as I noticed people watching and with my family's encouragement, I began to push myself. I wasn't going to quit. Before long, I was toughing it out and walking the whole way there. I wanted people to see me walking into that therapy room. I didn't want there to be a doubt in anyone's mind that I was ready to leave.

The walks inside the hospital got longer. On a couple of occasions, I went down to the coffee shop in the hospital with my mom and dad—the same place where they sat and wondered whether I was going to survive the night. Now I was joining them for lunch. And as I began moving around the hospital, everyone wanted to talk to me. I felt like the celebrity of the hospital.

"Look at Anthony go!" someone would yell as I walked by their station. "How ya doin', pal?" I could understand their enthusiasm.

The truth is, there aren't a lot of feel-good stories coming out of the burn unit. The staff members were proud of the job they'd done to save my life, and they were witnessing a recovery like they'd never seen. For the most part, I loved the attention. It gave me a purpose. It made me work harder, because I was a total ham. You think this is cool? Wait until you see what I can do next! I wanted to show people that I was like my Uncle Rick and Rocky Balboa. Nothing was going to stop me.

One other source of motivation was when former Pittsburgh Steeler running back Rocky Bleier would come to visit. Rocky was a four-time Super Bowl champ with the Pittsburgh Steelers—a true hero and for good reason.

Before he played in the Super Bowl, Rocky was drafted into the army and served in Vietnam. While he was on patrol, Rocky was shot in the left thigh by enemy fire. As he was down on the ground, a grenade sent shrapnel into his right leg and he lost part of his right foot. He received a Bronze Star and a Purple Heart for his heroism.

Doctors told Rocky he'd never play football again. He was even cut a few times by the Steelers. But every time, he came back and made the team, eventually becoming a starter.

Rocky took an interest in me and started showing up at my physical therapy sessions. As it turned out, he was starting a television show called *Fighting Back* and he wanted my story to be the first two episodes of the show. I admired Rocky; he'd done what I wanted to do. I wanted to come back and play football again.

Some of those physical therapy sessions that Rocky attended were torture. The remaining part of my amputated left hand was still incredibly swollen and a source of mind-numbing pain. At first, my therapist would touch it with a feather, and I would wail. Eventually, we got to the point where she could tap it with a spoon. Again, agony. She was trying to desensitize it so that even the simplest things like going for a car ride wouldn't be a journey in soul-crushing pain. But I endured it. Every stroke of the feather, every tapping of the spoon got me closer to the goal.

I had to learn how to use my right hand for everything. That meant tying my shoes with one hand. I did it repeatedly, until I could do it as fast as I once could with two hands.

I also had to use that hand to grab the railing as I pulled my way up a flight of stairs. I still couldn't bend my knees, so every time I lifted myself up to the next step, the pain vibrated through my body. It was a test that I refused to fail.

No detail for my return home was too small or overlooked. They even taught me how to remove the staples from my body. Imagine that—after each shower I learned to feel for staples and pull them out with a staple remover. Growing up, I wanted to be John Rambo and nothing made me feel more like a warrior than pulling those staples out.

Everything was painful, but I got used to enduring the pain because there really was no other choice. If the therapists asked me to lift a weight 5 times, I would try to lift it 20 times. I would push myself harder than ever.

There was one detail that was ever-present, pushing me forward. As I continued to work with the therapists, I was training with one other short-term goal in mind—to walk out of the hospital. No wheelchair. I wanted to hold my mom and dad's hands and walk out, just the way we promised each other I would.

Midway through January, a spot opened up for me at a local rehab center. The therapists felt I was walking and handling the daily activities well enough to get discharged. On January 14, the day I was set to be released, Dr. Goldfarb asked to see me in the conference room, the very same room where he sat with Dr. Slater on Halloween night as they told my parents that I likely wasn't going to survive my first night in the hospital. I walked to the conference room by myself.

"It wasn't so long ago that I was in this room with your parents," Dr. Goldfarb said. "And we had a much different conversation than the one I'm going to have with you today." He told me how proud he was of me. How strong I was. He said in his career, he had never seen someone who was as strong as I had to be in order to survive. I had made it through a lot.

"I'm not going to say it was you," he said. "And I'm not going to say it was me. There was definitely another force involved." I took that to mean that he was referring to God.

"But now, Anthony, my job here is done. You have to face the outside world. Now the ball is in your court. Who you become after this is a decision you have to make. Are you going to be in a wheelchair? Are you going to be limited in your mobility? Are you going to make it to the football field? These are all potential outcomes. You have to choose who you are going to be. So, every time it gets difficult at physical therapy or difficult at school, you have to think about who you want to be."

In that moment without hesitation or realization of how long a road was ahead, I looked Dr. Goldfarb in the eye and said,

"Oh, I'm going to play football. I'll be back." That conversation in the conference room with Dr. Goldfarb inspired me greatly. He let me know that he believed in me, and I never wanted to let him down. Every time I didn't feel like doing physical therapy, every time I felt lazy, Dr. Goldfarb's words would come back to me. He was the doctor who thought I had a chance. He believed that I could be the one in a million person who could survive all those risky cadaver skin procedures. If he felt making it to the football field was a possible outcome, then I had to do everything I could to get there.

As my family and I prepared to leave that day, the mood at the hospital was celebratory. The staff members organized a surprise party for me. Everyone there was glowing; we took pictures that I still have to this day. The kid who had a 0% chance of surviving, the one whose parents were supposed to be making funeral arrangements, the "snowball's chance in hell," was now going home. The staff members took pride in saving my life. They were part of a team that had proven the statistics wrong. Ten weeks seemed like a long time to be living in a hospital, but from where I was on Halloween to where I was now, I knew it was a miracle. It was a miracle that I was about to walk out on my own, and they had helped make it happen.

Only a few weeks ago, I listened to people say their last goodbyes as though I were dying. Now, people were visiting me and telling me how I inspired them, wishing me the very best. Now that I was getting ready to be released, it became quite the human-interest story. I was regularly being interviewed by the news media; I felt the prayers and support and it made me work even harder.

When it was time to go, it was as if the president of the United States was leaving West Penn. People were lining the hallways three-deep. They were clapping and cheering as I took the long walk step by step through the hospital, from my room to the discharge door (with an elevator ride in between). It was like a parade inside the hospital with balloons and everything. All of the news crews that had been covering my story were there to capture the moment—the boy who should have died was walking out of the hospital with his parents. It was covered in *USA Today* and newspapers around the world.

Although I'm a huge Steeler fan today, I wore my Washington Redskins track suit and hat—the team I was hoping would win the Super Bowl that year—and I soaked it all up as I made my way out of the hospital. Everyone at West Penn was so good to us; as a matter of fact, the hospital president and vice president themselves insisted on carrying my mother's suitcases to the car.

The challenge of walking out of the hospital was no small feat. I hadn't really walked that far yet, and it was very painful, but I looked at it as if it were a sporting event. When I got tired, I stopped to catch my breath. When I was thirsty, my mom gave me a drink, but I refused to sit down. There were so many people cheering me on, there was no way I was going to let them down.

One of the hospital staffers pushed a wheelchair right behind me in case I couldn't make it to the door. And as nice as it would have been to just sit down and ride out as quickly as possible, that wheelchair nipping at my heels was the added motivation. One foot in front of the other, I told myself. I promised my dad I was walking out of there. And, really, I promised myself. The pain is temporary, I kept repeating to myself.

The closer I got to the exit, the more determined I was to succeed. I can remember passing through the hospital's sliding doors, feeling the fresh winter air, the sunshine on my face. It was as though I had scored the winning touchdown in the Super Bowl. I hadn't had my opportunity to play under the lights at Taggart Stadium just yet, but this victory was by far the biggest win of our lives. I'll never forget embracing my mom, dad, and GeGe during this moment of glory. Dad said, "I told you we'd walk out of here together." I responded, "We keep our promises." And that we did.

13

Two Steps Back

AFTER WALKING OUT of West Penn, in my mind, I was ready to start running. My spirits were lifted by the hard work I put into getting back on my feet. But as desperately as I wanted to get home, New Castle still seemed farther away than it should. As soon as we left the hospital, we drove to a television studio to film interviews for the first two episodes of Rocky Bleier's *Fighting Back* show. With football on my mind, we then went straight to the Harmarville Rehabilitation Center, which was located a few miles outside of Pittsburgh. That was the place where the doctors at West Penn thought I would take the next step forward in my recovery, and I was willing to work my hardest to master everything I needed to do to live an independent life and regain my athletic form.

Once I was situated in my room, my parents and brother left. That was part of the deal at Harmarville; my family wasn't allowed to stay, and that made the transition very difficult for me. My support team who had been with me nonstop for two-and-a-half months were gone. In hindsight, I realized that part of the reason the doctors sent me to rehab was to give my family a break as well. They had been helping to care for me from the beginning. Whenever I would finally go home, they would be the ones who would have to care for me again without any support staff. When they left, I felt that loneliness immediately.

As I sat in the room alone, a familiar face wheeled himself in.

"My man!" Phillip Macri said.

I couldn't believe my eyes. Philip Macri was a New Castle legend. He was one of the best basketball players the town had ever seen. When I was in sixth grade, I went to the game when

New Castle played North Allegheny. It was Philip's junior season. As the clock expired, Philip hit a long buzzer beater to win the game. Division I colleges had already been swarming him. I'd heard that St. John's was eager to have him play for their school.

The previous August, Philip was in Virginia Beach for a baseball tournament. Just before he was headed home, he decided to go swimming in the ocean. When he went out for one last swim, he was hit by a huge wave, and he suffered a tragic spinal cord injury, leaving him a quadriplegic. Instead of pursuing college basketball glory and a scholarship, he would be confined to a wheelchair for the rest of his life.

Despite this cruel fate, Philip was all smiles and optimism. Witnessing his mental toughness taught me more than any words could say. I looked up to Philip and still do. I can never express how thankful I am for the time we shared at Harmarville. Philip would wheel himself into my room, and we would spend hours talking about life. I told him how I wanted to play football for New Castle, the next man up in the Razzano legacy. He told me he had no doubt that I could if I tried hard enough. Hearing that from someone I admired had a great impact on me.

I talked about playing football a lot during that time. And people would always tell me, "Of course, you can, Anthony! You can do anything you put your mind to!" But sitting here in the rehab center, I began to wonder if everyone was just telling me what they thought I wanted to hear.

Although the staff members were great, I felt out of place. It seemed to me that most of the other patients' athletic careers were behind them. My objective was to use this time in physical rehabilitation as a training camp to get back to the ballfield. I envisioned that my mornings would start with stretching, lifting, and physical activity. I envisioned myself getting stronger, faster, and more mobile. Harmarville was focused on addressing the things most pressing for rehabilitation patients: can you dress yourself, keep yourself clean? Can you get around your house without assistance?

After the strenuous rehab at West Penn, I felt those things were inevitable. My mind was on the future. Can I run? Can I jump? Can I tackle? But none of these questions were being asked at Harmarville. In their minds, I would be lucky to walk again. They told my father the days of a life where my knees bent and hips turned like they once did were gone. They told him I would never run again, so how could I expect to survive the physical trauma of high school tackle football? In their minds, other kids would break me if I didn't break myself first.

On most days at Harmarville, I would only spend one hour in physical therapy. The other 23 hours were spent sitting around talking. Those conversations did me a lot of good. I realized that I had an opportunity that some of the other patients might not. But due to the different nature of our health conditions, I needed to be far more active. During my stay, I could feel my body regressing. All the hard work I'd put in at West Penn to get on my feet was eroding by the hour. The less I moved, the less I could move. It was a downward spiral.

Mom and Dad tried to come as often as they could. I think Dad was there every other day. Every time they came, I would beg them to take me home. "This isn't the place for me," I told them. "I'm not getting better here." But they said we had to trust the doctors. The doctors knew what was best.

The lack of movement was causing my skin to fuse together. Walking was getting harder when it was supposed to be getting easier. It didn't help that I had a dropped foot—a condition that causes weakness and sometimes paralysis in your foot. Because I couldn't move my right foot, I had to wear a brace when I walked, which made me struggle that much more.

One day, my father was sitting next to my bed when he leaped up and exclaimed, "I saw your right foot move!"

I looked toward my foot at the end of the bed but couldn't see or feel anything.

"Do it again, son," he said.

Wanting to show him that he was crazy, I tried. And I tried. I tried to pull the top of my foot toward me. And sure enough, it moved slightly. It was the first time I could remember moving it since the accident.

"You're doing it! You're doing it," Dad said.

Did he actually see my foot move? Probably not. But he believed that he did. And he was able to transfer that belief to me. My dad's optimism helped keep me alive, and now it was helping me to move again.

It was a highlight of one of the darkest times in my life. After my dad left, I could feel a frustration growing within me. The joy I experienced leaving the hospital had been replaced with sadness, and I didn't know how to cope with it. I did everything they asked of me at West Penn so I could go home. And now they weren't asking enough of me at Harmarville. My father's overflowing optimism did more to help me than the hour of rehab I was doing each day. It felt like every step I was taking forward, I was also taking two steps backward.

One night, as I lay in the darkness while everyone slept, alone with my thoughts, I came to the stark realization that I needed to find a better way. I desperately missed the optimism that Dr. Goldfarb and the therapists at West Penn had for my future. I needed to be challenged in a way that pushed me to be the person I wanted to be. If I was going to get back to school, back on the football field, back to "normal," I was going to have to change course as soon as possible.

By the end of the second week at Harmarville, it felt like I was in a prison of limited beliefs. My room was a cell with occasional visitation rights. I had one hour in the yard for exercise therapy, and then it was back to my cell. When I was brought back to West Penn for a checkup with Dr. Goldfarb, I knew this was my only chance to escape. I had to plead my case to the one person who could do something about it.

When it came time to visit him, I didn't walk into his office. I was pushed in with a wheelchair. With my adhesions coming back stronger than ever, it was too painful to walk again.

"What happened to you?" Dr. Goldfarb asked. "The last time I saw you, you were walking out of here. What's the deal with the wheelchair?"

"I hate it there, doc," I said. "I'm going backwards. I only get one hour of therapy a day for my entire body. The rest of the time, I'm lying in bed."

"You're regressing," Dr. Goldfarb said. "We've got to get you out of there."

Much to my parents' surprise, the doctor suggested I return home and come back to West Penn for my rehabilitation. And while I'm sure my parents thought they were done with spending every day at West Penn, my mother dutifully made the hour-long drive there and back each day to take me to rehab, where the therapists redid all of their work to get me moving again.

When my mom came to check me out of Harmarville, I knew that this time I was finally going home. It couldn't have come a second sooner. I was physically and emotionally exhausted. I wanted to see my friends again. I wanted to go back to the life I once had, no matter how challenging it might be.

There was a celebration waiting for me back at my house. Family from all over came to welcome me back home. But before Mom took me home, she had one stop to make.

The Joy Gardens was a local bar in New Castle. "All of our friends are going to want to see you," she said. When we got inside, it seemed like half of New Castle was there to celebrate my arrival. Harmarville had felt like a prison and stopping at Joy Gardens on the way home only emphasized that. The party felt like a scene in *Goodfellas*, and I had just been sprung from the joint. (Ironically, the bar was later renamed Wise Guys.) I was so exhausted, I could barely stand up. As I sat at a side table while my mother and father laughed and entertained their friends, one of the guys came over and put a beer down in front of me.

"Here," he said to 12-year-old me. "You look like you need this."

I took one taste and practically spit it out. As grown up as I felt, all I wanted was a soda and a sandwich.

Once everyone at Joy Gardens had a chance to celebrate, I was finally taken home to the even bigger second party, where my family and friends were waiting. It was great seeing everybody, but I was worn out. It was a stark reminder that I wasn't the same kid anymore. I wasn't the super strong athlete that all the girls wanted to be around. I was so weak, I had to lie down on the couch. My dark skin had been replaced by a pale white pallor, as I was still recovering from months of surgeries and trauma.

Even before it was time for everyone to leave the house, I felt like all the energy had been drained from my body. It was too exhausting to stand up. And reality was beginning to set in. I couldn't go to sleep yet, because it was time to bathe, have my dressings changed, and put on my new pressurized Jobst garments. These garments were extremely tight, and they kept pressure applied to my entire body to help me heal. They were very difficult to put on, and I no longer had a team of people to help me do it. It was just me and Mom.

Fortunately, my Uncle Bob stayed behind to help. He was a giant of a man. He scooped me up and carried me upstairs to the tub. As I lay naked in the bath, I think it was the first time he really saw the true extent of my burns, and it was emotional for him. It was also still very painful for me to be in the tub. I knew it was hard on my Uncle Bob to experience that—what I looked like and how much pain I was in. It was also the first time we had been alone since the accident. When I was done in the bath, he carried me back downstairs, and then he told us that he had to leave. Emotionally, I think he was done. He couldn't be there anymore.

So now it was me and Mom again. Mom began applying the cream to my body and bandaging me before we started the daunting task of putting on the Jobst garments. I had only started wearing these garments the day before I left West Penn, so I didn't have much experience putting them on. When Mom started to try pulling them on my body, she was really struggling. It hurt a lot, and they weren't going on smoothly, which made me even more frustrated. And that's when I began to cry. Unlike the moments in physical therapy when I cried from the pain, in this situation, my mom sensed that I was crying because I felt bad for myself. So, instead of a tender kiss, she had to find the gumption to show me tough love, and that's exactly what she did.

In fact, she slapped me across the face. In Italian, we call this a *schiaffo*. She looked deeply in my eyes and said, "Anthony, you listen to me! You're not allowed to feel sorry for yourself! If you start feeling bad for yourself now, you'll be a victim for the rest of your life, and I love you too much for that!" She said all this as tears rolled down her face. She wasn't being cruel or mean. She was being honest and she was doing what she knew was best for me. Even though it broke her heart to slap me, it was a courageous thing to do and exactly what I needed in that moment.

So, I immediately started pulling up the Jobst garments with my right hand. I kept pulling and manipulating the garment until it began to cover my legs.

"See?" my mother said. "You see? You can do it yourself."

I also tied my shoes with my right hand for the first time. I should have been happy, but all I could feel was my frustration. It was the frustration that made me try harder. I know it was difficult for my mother to show me tough love in that moment. But now, I'm so happy she did. It was a spark that kept me fighting for independence, and without it, I might have stayed in that very spot.

14

Home Sweet Home

Now THAT I was home, I was desperately trying to find the new normal. That Sunday, Dad threw a Super Bowl party and my friends Artie and Johnny came over to watch the Washington Redskins defeat the Denver Broncos 42-10. I had never been happier to watch football in my life.

But no matter how hard I tried, getting back to a normal life continued to be elusive. After a few days at home, we began what turned out to be a long search for physical therapists to continue my rehab. I still went to West Penn, but it was difficult to make the commute every day. At first, we tried to have a therapist come to the house. The people were very nice, but it wasn't nearly the same. You could tell they were used to dealing with older people who were housebound and not young patients with burn injuries. They didn't have enough equipment. I often had to do the sessions on my living room floor. We knew right away it wasn't going to work.

Mom was dedicated to finding a solution, so we began driving to any physical therapy center near us in an effort to find the best spot for me. When I wasn't doing physical therapy, Mom would take me for walks at the mall. It was winter, and the mall was a big warm space for both of us. On those days, it was just the two of us, and we would spend a good part of the day walking and talking. We were making the most of it, and we became closer than ever.

The home phone kept ringing with requests for interviews as well. At the time, Sally Jesse Raphael had one of the biggest syndicated morning television shows watched by millions of people around the country. She was putting together an episode on "miracles" and asked my parents if I would be on the show.

143

What we didn't realize was a trip like this required a lot of sitting around—on the plane, in the hotel room, in the green room before the show, on stage in front of an audience. All that inactivity was eroding the steady progress I had been making.

After only two days, I started having issues doing simple things like standing up. When we got off the plane from New Haven, I couldn't stand up on my own. My parents rushed me from the airport straight to West Penn Hospital. The doctors told me I needed surgery right away because my skin was fusing together in all the wrong places.

Imagine having open wounds on the back of your knees. That's what it felt like for me. When I sat in the same position for a long time, it was as if the skin from my thighs was attaching itself to the skin on my calves, because that was the closest place for it to attach itself and grow.

At West Penn, Dr. Newton was one of the best microsurgeons in the world. He put together a three-year plan involving some of the most complex surgeries that, in theory, would allow me to regain my mobility.

Because of all that scar tissue and how tight it was, it looked as if my body was hunched over all the time. Dr. Newton inserted balloons on both my shoulders that he would fill with saline. Each week, I would go back to West Penn, and he would insert more saline to gradually allow my skin to expand. Once it had expanded, he would then cut out some of the scar tissue and stretch my newly grown skin over the area. Over time, this started to give me more flexibility in my joints. Each time, I would have to stay in the hospital for a few days until they were sure that all my blood vessels, arteries, and veins had been reattached precisely and there were no complications.

The idea of continually getting sliced open was difficult. Going back to the hospital all the time was exhausting for everyone. I trusted the doctors and knew that without these procedures, I would never get the range of motion my body needed to play football again. It was a commitment I needed to make.

After a few weeks of physical therapy and with some of the new surgical procedures completed, I was beginning to move better, and everyone thought maybe it would be best if I went back to school. My closest friends had been coming around the house already and spending time with me.

I was excited to get back to school. In my mind, despite the accident and the current state of my health, I was the same kid who left school in November. Being able to go there every day and see my friends would be one step closer to "normal," one step closer to being myself again.

One of my first classes was physical education. I wasn't afraid of it, but it wasn't exactly how I wanted to start back at school either. The class was playing a version of baseball where a kid would pitch a volleyball in, and you would have to hit it with a Wiffle Ball bat. That excited me because I was a very good baseball player, so I was confident I could do it, even with one hand.

When my turn came, the pitch came toward me and with the bat in my right hand, I slugged the ball hard. As soon as I hit it, I dropped the bat and motored to first base. I reached first base safely, and I was proud that I was back! Anthony Razzano had returned! And that's when I looked around and saw that everything in the gym had come to a standstill. Everyone's eyes were staring at me.

I'm not sure what the other kids were thinking when they saw me running, but it was clear they were curious enough to stop whatever they were doing to watch me hobble stiff-legged to first base. Even the kid who fielded the ball stood there with the ball in his hand. He never threw it to first base. I would have easily been out if he did.

It was the worst feeling of all—a feeling of disappointment. In my mind, I was cruising down to first base as naturally as I always did. But you could see it in their expressions: nothing was the same anymore. I was used to being a good baseball player. Now, kids who didn't even play organized baseball were better than me.

"Good job," one of them said, patting me on the shoulder. I hated it. The pity of people feeling sorry for me. From a psychological standpoint, that was the moment I embraced the idea of getting more surgical procedures. If there were any way to get me back to where I wanted to be faster, sign me up. I knew I wasn't going to last at school if my movement—and the kids' reactions—were going to be like this all the time.

I wanted to get back to normal, but this wasn't normal, at least not to me. Getting around from class to class, going up and down stairs, dealing with the rigors of being in a rush with 500 other kids to not be late—it became overwhelming. Maybe I didn't want to admit it at the time, but I wasn't ready. My body wasn't ready to sit still for hours each day in an uncomfortable desk chair. When you're a healthy seventh grader, you don't think about getting through an overcrowded hallway, of having to move at the same pace or faster than everyone else. So I decided that maybe it was best to pack it in for the school year. My priority was no longer math, geography, and science.

My priority was coming back to school as Anthony Razzano. And the only way I was going to do that was to have the surgeries and rehabilitation and give myself a chance to heal properly so I could come back as the person I wanted to be.

I wasn't the only Razzano home from school. GeGe had deferred the semester as well and was going to reenroll in college in the fall. That gave us the opportunity to spend a lot more time together.

GeGe wasn't just my brother; he was my closest friend. I told him everything, even the stuff I wouldn't share with anyone else. One night, I was talking to GeGe about how much I wanted to play baseball and football again. I missed the competition and physicality of it. But I also admitted to him that I wasn't sure I would be able to do it. I had tried playing catch with a baseball a few days before. I was hoping to start playing right away. But after that game of catch, it was abundantly clear that I wasn't ready. Maybe I would never be ready.

"It's not whether or not you can do it," GeGe said. "You have to do it."

"What if I can't?" I asked.

"Look, you're just not doing enough," GeGe said.

It took me by surprise. I was doing everything the doctors and therapists asked me to do. I was even doing extra walking around the mall. Nothing was easy for me. Going up and down the house stairs was torture.

Then GeGe looked at me with disdain and said, "You know there are people who have it more difficult than you, right?"

"What?" I said. "Who?"

"Do you forget being at Harmarville?" GeGe said. "If those kids could walk, they wouldn't be complaining about not being able to move or feeling sorry and doubting themselves. You have to believe in yourself. They never thought you would make it out of West Penn, did they?"

"No," I said.

"But you walked out of there, didn't you?"

"Yes."

"So you have to quit listening to other people's opinions about what you can or cannot do and realize that you have to give it your all every single day, and everything will fall into place."

When GeGe told me that, it hit me right between the eyes. I thought I had been moving around, trying to get better, but what had I really been doing? Walking around in the mall? The pain I experienced wasn't necessarily equal to my effort, let alone the results. I reflected on the time at Harmarville and realized that the patients with spinal cord injuries had it much more difficult than me. I thought about Philip Macri's attitude, how he was always smiling, and decided to try and be more like him.

There was a fitness club down the street from our house called The Club Fitness Center. Our family friend, Leslie Sansone, was a famous fitness instructor. She had created best-selling fitness videos and was the owner of the gym. She had offered me a lifetime club membership to work out anytime I wanted.

Lying in bed that night, I asked GeGe if he would take me there the next day, and he did.

When we first walked into the gym, it was comforting that it didn't seem that much different than the therapy room at West Penn. They had a lot of the same pulley machines. I began experimenting with those first, because they were familiar to me.

Eventually, I got the courage to try the bench press on the Nautilus machine. I wasn't used to doing something with both arms since my left hand had been amputated. The machine allowed me to move the bar without worrying about dropping it on myself. I wasn't sure how difficult it would be to lift and lower the bar without gripping it with both hands. The remaining part of my left hand was still terribly painful, but I pushed through. I wasn't using very much weight at first, but I could feel the difference in my body almost immediately. It was as if the muscles I hadn't used since before the accident had started to wake up.

I used the leg extension machine the most. While seated, you lift a weighted bar with your shins. I was still having issues with the skin contracting behind my knees, and the skin on the fronts of my kneecaps had hardened, which made it excruciating to lift the weight. Every time I finished the exercise, blood would seep from an open wound.

But that blood was a badge of honor. The results were hard to deny. Eventually, I had enough mobility in my legs to begin riding a bike around my neighborhood. This newfound freedom was a breath of fresh air.

One afternoon, as I was riding home, I saw a big red van in the driveway, which I knew meant one thing: Uncle Rick was here! He was back in town to host his annual football camp in New Castle, and that always lifted my spirits. When I ran into the house, there he was with one of his best friends, Anthony Muñoz. Anthony was one of the greatest offensive linemen in NFL history. He was Uncle Rick's former teammate from the Cincinnati Bengals. They were roommates at training camp and for away games. From those experiences, they became the best of friends. By extension, we all got to know him very well; he was a friend of the family.

But this was the first time he had seen me since the accident, and I could see the sadness in his face. I wasn't that little boy running around the locker room during the Super Bowl anymore. I was a soon-to-be teenager with a badly burned body. Anthony talked to me and fired me up that day. He encouraged me to keep trying to play football, and he was excited about the camp the next day.

The following morning, Uncle Rick picked me up and drove me to the camp as was our tradition every year, but this year was very different. In past years, I was one of the star players in my age group. I would be all over the field. But despite all the progress I was making in the gym, it was clear that I wasn't ready to play football yet. Instead of being on that field as one of the best players, I had to sit by the goalpost and watch the other kids play. It was a stark reminder of how far away I was from ever playing football again. The camp, which used to make me one of the happiest kids in the world, made me feel more depressed than ever before.

That afternoon, I sat on the patio of my mother's house, and I was despondent. About an hour later, my dad drove by to pick me up because he was bringing me to stay with him that night. He came strolling up to the patio in a black pinstriped three-piece suit. That was Dad; he loved to look sharp. Even if he didn't have anywhere to go, he was going to dress the part.

When Dad asked me about my day, I told him about the camp and how sad it made me.

"You know, you're not improving fast enough," he said. "You're going to need to start doing push-ups."

"Dad, my hand," I said, pointing to my left hand. "How am I supposed to do push-ups like this?"

"Then do one-armed push-ups," he said.

"Are you crazy? How am I supposed to do one-armed push-ups?"

And so my dad, the 38-year-old guy who was dressed like Clark Gable, got down on all fours on the patio in the Pennsylvania summer sun and proceeded to do 25 push-ups with his right arm, followed by 25 push-ups with his left.

"If I can do them, you can do them. Try," he said.

Dutifully, I got off the chair and placed my right hand and feet on the ground in a tripod position, and I slowly lowered my 12-year-old body down, grimacing and straining until I went back up and my right arm was extended straight again. That was one. I managed to squeeze out three more before I couldn't do anymore.

But that wasn't the point my dad was trying to make. It wasn't that I couldn't do 50. He knew that. It was that I could do one, and I didn't know that. And once I learned that I could do it,

I tried and tried every day. Eventually, I got to 25. I was even able to do some on my left hand as well.

Everything that GeGe and my dad were trying to tell me started to sink in. I thought I was working hard at the gym. Maybe it was because the exercises that I was doing were painful at times. Or maybe I allowed myself to put limitations on what I thought I could do because of my missing left hand. But that all had to end. I might have been working hard enough to be a kid who could shuffle from class to class, holding his own books. But it wasn't enough if I wanted to be a student athlete chasing down ballcarriers and dragging them to the ground. That was going to require a bigger effort than I'd made up to that point.

I never wanted to be the kid who sat by the goalpost again. I wanted to be the kid on the field tackling people like my Uncle Rick did. The Razzanos had a reputation in New Castle of being the hardest workers on the football field. If I was going to get there myself, I not only had to uphold that reputation but also I was going to have to surpass it.

15

Ocean City

SOMETIMES WE LOOK back on our lives and the path we should have taken is so clear. And typically, we don't get second chances, which can lead to regret. During my darkest days in the hospital, all we wanted as a family was a second chance and that's not something we took for granted. So, as life continued to unfold, I knew that I only had one shot and I had to give it everything if I was going to get where I wanted to be. Growing up, no matter what the sport, I hated to lose. The thought of not being the person I wanted to be was what fueled me. But before I could fully recover physically, I needed to get my spirit back, find the person I used to be.

It started with accepting my new physical reality—both within my body and my home. In addition to my athletic capabilities, I was also adjusting to the idea that no matter how close my mother and father were in the hospital, ultimately, things were going to return back to the way they were before the accident. Dad and Mom were both in their own relationships now. But that didn't prevent them from wanting to have a deeper relationship with me, and this was something that continued to heal my heart and mind.

Dad, his girlfriend, and their one- and two-year-old kids had moved to a house that was closer to my school and to Taggart Stadium. He made a big bedroom for me in the upper level of the house. If there was a big movie coming out, Dad always took me to see it. If I wanted a pack of baseball cards, Dad would buy a whole box. He was still there for me, encouraging me to keep getting healthier and back to the life I wanted. He even put a heavy bag in the basement for me to work out with and bought me my first set of weights.

Mom had gone back to work at the beauty salon. Money may have been tight, but it never felt as if we couldn't do what we wanted to do if it meant something to us.

The previous summer, my Aunt Marilyn invited me on vacation with her and her family to Ocean City, Maryland. It was a magical trip for me. It was my first time visiting the ocean, and I loved everything about it. As you drove over the Bay Bridge into Ocean City, you could smell the salt water and feel the mist as it breezed through the open windows of the car. With only one glance, you could see the entire length of the town, from the surfers on the tail end of the beach to the Ferris wheel that punctuated the amusement park. There was a sense of peace and happiness in Ocean City that did not exist in my everyday life. How I longed to feel that peace again.

During the months at West Penn, Mom reflected on my time at the beach and promised herself that if I survived, we would start making those types of memories together. So, that summer, she was determined to do just that. When the opportunity presented itself, we joined Mom's closest friend Gracie and her kids and took the long drive to the beach for a weeklong stay.

I was so excited for the trip. I would tell my mom how the air just smelled different there, and she would listen intently as I described the joy I felt from playing in the ocean the summer before. Mom bought me a long-sleeved swim shirt and long swim pants to cover the Jobst garments. In these clothes, walking around on the beach, I didn't look that much different from the surfers that were ascending out of the water in their wetsuits.

By this point, I was moving around better. I was still a bit hunched over; the surgeries hadn't fully straightened my posture yet. I was able to walk from place to place well enough, but I hadn't really tested out what it was like to swim. Before we left, the doctors made it clear that the salt water from the ocean might not feel all that pleasant on my recovering skin, even if I was covered from head to toe with the Jobst garments.

Despite that, the doctors were fine with me wading into the rough waves. In Ocean City, I could have easily sat on the sidelines, and no one would have given me a hard time about it—least of all, my mother, who was worried about me handling the unforgiving currents of the ocean.

But the excitement from last year's vacation inspired a hope in me to get back out there. I just couldn't wait to feel the waves break over my head and the cool breeze touch my sun-kissed face.

When we got to Ocean City, Mom bought me a boogie board. They were the most popular thing to have on the beach. The smaller kids would use it as a way to float along the shoreline. The teenagers would wade out into the ocean with it, and when a big wave came, dive on top of the board and ride the wave to the shore.

Without having two hands to grip the board, and with the ocean current being rough at times, riding the board became a puzzle to solve. This was the delicate line my mother was learning to straddle. She wanted me to be like all the other kids, having fun in the ocean. But would I be able to handle it? Would it get too dangerous for me? She stood a lot closer to the shoreline and watched me as I stepped into the water.

After gripping the board a few different ways, I discovered if I wrapped my right arm completely around the board and used my right hand to grip the left side of the board, then the board stayed locked in tight. When that first wave came in, I dove onto the board with it firmly in my grasp and let the cool water wash over me as the wave propelled me back toward the shore where Mom was standing.

That cool ocean water felt glorious. It may have burned in certain places on my body, but I took the sting as a badge of courage. Here in the Atlantic Ocean, I didn't feel like the disabled kid who couldn't play. I felt like myself again. Swimming had become a medicine for my body and my soul.

Each day that went by, my confidence grew in the ocean. Soon, I was fighting waves face forward, as if I were a linebacker, and when a big wave came toward shore, I would launch myself into it as though I was tackling a ballcarrier.

My mom called me a fish because I stayed in the water from sunup until dinner. Physically, I felt my range of motion getting a little better each day, but it was so much more than that. My hair was now jet black again and I was regaining that dark Italian brown skin tone—I was getting my looks back. When I looked in the mirror, I could see myself again, the way I remembered myself—the popular kid, the one that girls wanted to talk to. Each day brought a new wave of healing, a newfound confidence; I began to remember how I used to be. It was as if the ocean water was a baptism of sorts ushering me into my new life.

That swagger began to manifest itself away from the ocean as well. After so many months in the hospital, I wanted to be part of the action again. One night, when Mom and her friend Gracie had stepped out for a minute, I snuck a beer out of the refrigerator with Gracie's son Gooch, who was the same age as me. We went outside behind the condo, away from watchful eyes, and we drank it together. It tasted so much better than the beer my parents' friends tried to give me when I came home from the hospital. Maybe it was because I wasn't supposed to be drinking it. Maybe that's what it tasted like to be free to become myself again. It wasn't bitter; it was refreshing in the night air. Gooch and I were just two 12-year-old boys having fun on vacation, making a memory that I'm sure we will both cherish forever.

In the evenings, Mom and I would stroll along the boardwalk and get something to eat. On one of the last nights of our trip, Mom wanted to take me to a nice restaurant for dinner, so she drove me up to Rehoboth Beach in Delaware, where we found a sweet little spot to have a quiet meal. Typically, Mom was frugal, but for whatever reason that night, she decided that money was not a concern. If I wanted to have the shrimp cocktail as an appetizer, I could. If I wanted to have ice cream for dessert, maybe we could each get one? She was determined not to let this moment pass. For the first time in our lives, we both now recognized that moments like these are to be cherished because we may never get them back.

During that dinner, we talked and laughed, just the two of us. There was no arguing between her and Dad. GeGe wasn't there to haze me and give me a tough time. It was just us, at dinner, without conditions. I could never remember us having a moment quite like this before. As much as I savored the food, I savored the laughter and the peace even more.

After dinner, our stomachs joyfully full, we went for a walk on the Rehoboth Beach boardwalk. As we passed the carnival games, we came across a glass booth that faced the boardwalk where people could sing karaoke. Strangers would walk by and see some well-meaning person in the booth, headphones on, listening intently to the music as they followed the words on the screen in front of them. And the resulting song, for better or worse, was broadcast outside for passersby to hear.

When Mom saw this, she coaxed me into giving it a shot. After all, I was fearless in the ocean. Why not on the board-walk? I was not a gifted singer. Getting up in front of complete strangers and singing a full song terrified me. But Mom made a special request. She wanted me to sing Whitney Houston's "The Greatest Love of All." It was a song she would sing to me often. In fact, I'd heard her sing it so many times, I probably didn't even need the screen with the lyrics. We both loved that song and the meaning behind the lyrics. Later in life, we would dance to it on my wedding day.

"Try it, Anthony," she said. "No one is here. It's just me."

As I looked around, I realized she was right—there really wasn't anyone standing around listening to the singers, and after the wonderful dinner we'd just had, how could I deprive her of this? Nervously, I entered the booth and put on the headphones. The music started, and the first lines of the lyr-ics came on the screen. I looked out the booth window to see Mom standing by herself, watching and listening, as most of the other people walked by.

As my cracking 12-year-old adolescent voice began sing-ing, the words rolled quietly off my lips. I started to feel the meaning of the song flow through my body, and my voice got stronger. The song is so powerful—about how children are the future and how their laughter reminds adults of how they used to be—and my mother began to cry. What started as a small tear turned into an emotional outpouring of love. There are some moments in life that are so special, so meaningful, and so filled with love that they can only be a grace from God above. This was one of those beautiful moments.

Maybe it was my mother's crying, maybe it was the sight of me in the booth, or maybe it was the crack in my 12-year-old voice, but it didn't take long for a crowd to begin forming around her. And when the spectators assembled, they saw a boy who had been badly burned, standing in his Jobst garments, holding the microphone in his one functional hand, singing about never walking in anyone's shadows and how no one could take away his dignity. And they started to cry, too. It was as though everyone knew the pain we had gone through and soon they were arm in arm swaying to the music, singing along with me. There was not a dry eye, including my own.

In one way, it felt like the longest 4 minutes and 51 seconds of my life; in another way, it felt like I released all of the pain stored in my soul in those few minutes. I cried, but I continued to sing, and the wounds in my soul healed, ones that I didn't even know were there. When I finished the song, I received a nice ovation from the people who had gathered to listen. The owner gave me a cassette recording of my efforts, which Mom was sure to play to all our family members when we returned home. It's a memory that we will treasure forever.

Regardless of how we got there, it was a miracle that I was still alive. Somehow, God allowed me to survive the unsurvivable. With my mother's encouragement, I stood up in a public place and didn't care about how people thought I looked or if they felt sorry for me. Their applause was nice, but it wasn't important. I wasn't singing the song for them. I wasn't even singing it for myself. I was singing it for her. This was the moment she wanted to have with me. She wanted to hear the words of that song come out of my mouth for the world to hear—that discovering how to love yourself is "the greatest love of all." My mom taught me that and that would be the springboard for every next step I'd take in my life.

16

It Takes a Village

WHEN I RETURNED home from Ocean City, I felt different about myself. I'd learned how to smile again, and now it was time for me to learn how to start living again. Even though my body was still recovering, I was never going to use that as an excuse to place a limit on myself. Fighting those waves prepared me to deal with the ups and downs that are part of growing up. Thankfully, I was blessed with a support system like no other.

The summer before eighth grade, Artie asked if I wanted to play golf with him. I hadn't played much before my accident, but my dad and brother played and would take me with them. I always had a knack for competitive sports, but this would present a new challenge. GeGe let me use his clubs and off I went. Artie's mom would drop us off at Sylvan Heights Golf Course with the agreement that she would come back later in the afternoon to pick us up.

Learning how to play golf with one hand put my determination to the test. Golf is a difficult sport to play well in perfect health. It requires an enormous amount of concentration and patience. At first, I could barely hit the ball, but I was relentless. I would spend countless hours learning how to swing the club with just my right hand. At first, I would draw the club back a quarter of the way and swing through with my sand wedge—the club that allowed me to get the ball in the air the easiest. I had to learn how to rotate my hips slightly, while keeping my head down and gain the feel of hitting the ball pure at contact.

We would go down to the bullpen at Sylvan Heights with a shag bag and hit balls for hours. I was slowly learning how to control the club to get the ball in the air. Once I started hitting my wedge flush, I moved on to hitting a seven-iron

165

off a tee. The key was to rotate my body in rhythm, with my left hand on the club, and focus on shoulder rotation. I got addicted to golf and everything about it, especially chipping and putting. Every day in that bullpen I would take advice on how to approach the game, how to swing under control, and how to lower my score. There were local golfers at Sylvan Heights such as Wynn Hasson, Danny Mangino, Ralphie Litrenta, and Albert and Johnny Dimuccio who would take the time to teach us kids how to swing and how to play the game right.

Sometimes in life the smallest piece of advice can make the biggest difference. Danny Mangino, who was just a few years older than me, was a great golfer and was hitting balls in the bullpen next to me. I was struggling at the time and he was hitting every shot perfectly. I stopped hitting shots for a minute just to watch him. He asked me what I was doing, and I told him that I wasn't sure if I'd ever be able to hit the ball like him. He looked at me and pointed around the golf course and said, "You see all these guys? What's the one thing they have in common?" I didn't know how to answer. He said, "They couldn't hit the ball when they got started; you are no different." And he leisurely walked to the tee to play his round.

That moment inspired me in a way that I can't quite express. I realized that I had to take the tools given to me and work with them if I wanted to get good. In one respect, it would become a motto for my life.

Soon, I began to develop a feel for the swing, for hitting the ball flush, and my game started coming together. Practicing this swing over and over helped me learn how to get my hips and legs into the swing. The time I spent chipping and putting every day helped me develop an incredible touch around the green. I may not have been able to drive the ball as far as I could've with two hands, but the closer I got to the green, the better I was.

As my game progressed, I was invited to play with the 12 o'clock crew at Sylvan Heights daily. The older guys at the golf course would organize something called a *squatsome*. Everyone would gather and put five bucks in a hat. Names were drawn and you were put in a foursome.

Oftentimes, I would get put with one of the older guys such as Buff Litrenta and his brother Red. The Rat Pack had nothing on these guys. As young men, Buff and Red were lifeguards in Las Vegas when the city started coming to life in the 1950s. They knew Frank Sinatra, Dean Martin, and all the heavy hitters from the early days of Vegas. The Litrenta boys brought that swagger back home to Pennsylvania with them.

Every day on the course with them and some of the other experienced golfers was a lesson in life. Playing with the older guys, you had to learn quickly, because there were no "gimmes." Everyone wanted to win and collect the cash. For the young guys, if you lost the five bucks in your pocket over the first nine holes, it meant you might be walking to McDonald's with no money for lunch. If someone took pity on you, they'd front you a buck to get something off the dollar menu.

I loved every minute on that golf course. Playing golf did wonders for my body. It required me to use my core to turn and swing. I'd have to bend over constantly to pick up the ball. It felt like a full body workout to me. But most of all, I loved competing again. It got my juices flowing. It made me feel like I belonged. I was one of the boys.

During one squatsome, I was paired with Buff. He told the group, "Anthony, my boy, is going to need an extra two strokes per side."

I was disappointed. I thought I was getting better at the game. I may not have been as good as the experienced golfers, but I was holding my own. I was even starting to make some pars, something I'd never done prior to the accident. And here was someone I admired asking for additional strokes for me.

When we got to the cart, Buff tapped me on the knee and said, "Did you see what I did there? I got you more than you needed."

"What do you mean?" I asked.

"Anthony, my boy, you must always remember this. The bet is always won at the first tee."

And that was my first business lesson on the golf course. In any business negotiation, how successful it will turn out for you is determined at the point of the negotiation. You don't succeed your way into a better deal; you negotiate a better deal that enables you to succeed. This was one of the many lessons I learned playing golf at Sylvan Heights. The camaraderie those men showed me made me feel welcome. They treated me as one of their own. It was up to me to live up to the faith they had in me.

Then about the same time in my life, I met one of the greatest people I'd ever know, Norman Moses. Norman lived down the street from my mom. He had a stand-alone garage and made a pool room out of it. Norman was the CEO of the Association for Responsible Care, an organization that advocated for kids with disabilities. Beyond that, Norman was actively involved in local politics. He probably helped more judges get elected than anyone in the history of Lawrence County politics. And despite how involved he was in the community, his greatest gift to New Castle may have been the pool room he created in his garage on Elizabeth Street, where he taught us the game and helped us develop street smarts at the same time.

I was a little nervous the first time I walked over to the garage, but Norman made me feel right at home.

"Anthony, my boy!" he greeted me.

"Hello, Mr. Moses," I said.

"Please, call me Norm." And for the next five years, until I went off to college, Norm's garage became both a second home, as well as an institution of higher learning for me.

Each day after school, I would meet up with my friends, and we'd walk down the street to Norm's garage. By about 6 p.m. or so, Norman would arrive home and join "his boys" as we all shot 9-ball together.

Norm taught us lessons playing pool that would serve us all very well in life. On day one, he taught me how to hold the cue stick and use my left hand as a bridge. He would always tell me, "Anthony, my boy, it's good to have a plan, but the key to life is how you improvise." His best lessons were taught to us by playing 9-ball, the style of game that the best pool players played. Norm taught us everything, but every lesson was grounded in maintaining focus, following a strategy, and, most important, thinking quickly on your feet.

The object of 9-ball is to sink each numbered ball in order until you ultimately sink the 9-ball to win the game. When you're a young inexperienced player as I was, you go from plan A to making a new plan A. Sink the 1-ball first. Then worry about where the 2-ball is.

Norm taught me that 9-ball was all about positioning, or the *po* as he liked to call it. Once you made your shot, where were you leaving the cue ball for your next shot? He taught me how to hit the cue ball hard in the center to make it stop as soon as it hit the object ball. Or sometimes, you needed to strike the top of the cue ball so that it would continue rolling in that direction to be in a better spot for the next shot. But my favorite action to put on the cue ball was the draw. Low English would cause the cue ball to back up after you hit the object ball. However, nothing made a difference in winning the game as much as having the proper touch—not hitting the cue ball too hard or too soft. It was all about execution and self-control.

And then, there were times where there wasn't a realistic next shot. In those cases, you had to play more defensively. If you couldn't sink the next ball, you had to make sure you left the cue ball in a place where your opponent couldn't make their shot either. To become good at 9-ball, you had to think two or three shots ahead. And that was true in life. How is what you are doing now going to affect the next thing you do? Are you leaving yourself in a good position? Or are you setting yourself up to fail? Norm would talk you through a game of pool, and by listening it taught us how to think for ourselves.

All that time on the golf course translated well to the pool table. The touch that I learned with my wedge and putter served me well with the pool cue. Once I learned the fundamentals of the game, I was beginning to make the cue ball do what I needed it to do.

As we shot pool, Norm loved talking local politics with us. He explained how to get things done in New Castle. It was a master class in local government, much better than any university could have provided.

Norm taught us how to think, strategically. The time he invested in us taught us street smarts and how to be one of the guys. We were learning about what to expect as adults and how we could help shape our own futures. Inevitably, my friends and I started betting on games; everyone wanted to win. Learning how to win is one of the great lessons of my life. But, even more important than that, was the greatest investment lesson I ever learned: you never bet more than you can afford to lose.

The best part about it was translating those lessons into other areas of my life as well. Whether it was Thursday night dances, Friday nights at high school games, or just hanging out on a corner all over town, we knew how to handle ourselves because of the lessons we learned in the pool hall.

But there was one itch I still had left to scratch.

As the autumn weather started to blow in, pickup football returned to Rose Avenue, the field I played on with GeGe and the boys before my accident. I'll never forget the day; it was a Saturday afternoon. I was leaving the Pop Warner games and walking to my dad's house with my friend Shawn Panella.

"Ant, it's time, man," Shawn said. "We need another player at the sandlot. You have to play football with us."

"I'm not sure," I said.

"You're doing everything else. Come down. Give it a shot," Shawn said.

With his encouragement, I decided to give it a try. I was a lot stronger and able to carry myself by this point, but I wasn't sure if I was ready. I was running more upright, but physically I was nowhere near myself again yet, even after all the surgical procedures. I could compete in golf and pool, but how would my body hold up getting thrown to the ground? I wasn't fast, but I had never been fast. That wasn't my game. I was a hard-nosed competitor and street smart on the field.

The first game back, it became clear right away that no one was going to take it easy on me. It turns out my biggest impediment wasn't running, but the pain in my amputated left hand. It was still very sore, especially when it came into contact with the ball.

After that game, I went home and found the pads I used to wear inside my catcher's mitt. I put one pad on the back of my left hand and one on the front. Then I took a glove that receivers use and cut the fingers off and sewed up the holes. I slid the glove over the pads, and now I had a little makeshift protective gear for my hand that took away a lot of the pain. It became much easier to catch the ball as well. I improvised! Norm was proud to hear about the adjustments I made.

There was something about competition that always brought out the best in me. Sure, I was making progress with rehab and working out. But by playing football nearly every day, my body started to change. Having to catch and defend passes, I was able to start lifting my arms directly over my head to reach for thrown footballs. My knees began bending more as I had to dig deep to chase down people carrying the football.

After playing games every day for a few weeks, I remember a particular day in November. We'd had an early snow, which made playing football even more fun. During the game, I had a play at running back and took a short pitch to the right side of the line. I was able to slip out of the defender's tackle and darted for the sideline. As I turned up field, I was sure someone was on my heels, so I ran like I was being chased by a crazed dog. All I could see was the end zone as I hit a stride like I never knew before. I found a new gear in that moment and what do you know? It led me all the way to the end zone. Touchdown!!

It was my first touchdown since before the accident and it felt so good. As I was running toward the goal line, I couldn't help but flash back to when I asked Henry Hartman if I could play ball after he put out the fire. I thought of the moments in the Jameson ER when I asked Mom if I could play in the game, and yes, I thought of how it felt on my first day back at school when my classmates' jaws dropped at the sight of my struggle. I knew it was only a sandlot game, but I also knew that no one let me score and I had everything I needed to take it to the next level.

In that moment, I set my sights a bit higher, I knew I could take every lesson I learned on the golf course, in the pool room, and on the sandlot and make a comeback to play varsity football. If I could do it here at Rose Avenue, there wasn't anyone that was going to stop me from living my dream and suiting up for the New Castle Red Hurricanes.

And if I was going to play for New Castle, I would be doing so under Lindy Lauro, the head coach and one of the greatest high school football coaches in history. If I wanted to play, I had to earn it.

In order to do so, I had to believe what Danny Mangino told me on the golf course: I was no different than anyone else. I had to take a page out of Buff's lessons and outsmart my opponents and, most important, I had to incorporate my lessons from Norman Moses: think strategically, put yourself in the right position, improvise, and be under control.

They say "it takes a village to raise a child," and I believe that to be true. My mentors prepared me for the idea that life wasn't always going to be fair. So, if I wanted an opportunity, I had to be the hardest-working person in the room and I had to get after it. It was time to take it to the next level, and I was ready for that challenge!

17

And His Hair Was Perfect

Growing up in a small town in Western Pennsylvania, there are certain rites of passage in a young man's life. As you become a teenager, you are trying to find the foundation of your identity. When I had my accident, it disrupted that process for me. I was on my way to becoming Anthony Razzano: star athlete. After the accident, to many people, I was Anthony Razzano: the kid who miraculously survived. This new identity brought me a level of New Castle fame like no other teenager. If I went to a high school football game, a crowd of people would gather around me as though I were a celebrity. And though I was flattered by the attention I was receiving, I didn't want it for just being at the game. I wanted it for being on the field.

Some of that attention came from girls my age and even older. My time in Ocean City helped me gain confidence talking to girls after the accident. When chatting on the boardwalk, I learned how to connect with people by being genuine, showing interest in them, and always smiling, especially with my eyes. I still didn't know how people would react to my scars, but I discovered a very important truth when meeting people on the boardwalk: most people are kind and are interested in others who are sincere, loving human beings. We are all flawed, so people look past the scars if they connect with you on another level.

When the junior high prom rolled around, I started to hear that one of the coolest girls in school wanted to go with me. She also had one of the coolest names: Angelic. So we started talking and formed what would become one of my closest lifelong friendships. We decided to go to the dance together.

Our parents made a big deal about the junior high prom. Angelic looked like a princess, and I was decked out in a tuxedo with tails, a top hat, and a cane. We went with another couple and rode in a black Cadillac with a driver.

Angelic and I had the time of our lives that night. We left the dance and went to a restaurant called the Boat House with a group of kids. We had so much fun, we ate good food, and we danced and partied like we were much older.

From that moment on, Angelic and I grew very close. She had a way about her; I just knew she was someone I could confide in. We shared a closeness that I now know is rare to find in life. We would meet up at parties every weekend and talk on the phone for hours. As time went on, we had so much fun doing all different kinds of things together. I taught her how to drive, even though she was only 15. Yeah, we got caught by her Aunt DeAnne, but we made her promise not to tell.

Angelic would even join me when I went to Norm's garage to shoot pool. My boys weren't too crazy about that either. But the way I looked at it, Angelic was welcome around me no matter where I was.

One day after school, Angelic came home with me and we decided to walk over to Norman's to hang out. When we got there, we discovered the lock had been changed. At first, I thought Norman was closing down the garage. But then my boys showed up and went right in. As it turned out, my friends did it because they wanted it to be guys only.

So Angelic decided to write Norman a letter. We went back to my house and wrote it up like it was a complaint being filed to the court. When Norman got home, we headed down to the house. Angelic wrote the letter but made me promise to do all the talking, so I did. Norman loved it, and I'll never forget the peculiar words he said when he read the letter and I finished my presentation. He just looked up at me and said, "And his hair was perfect" in his distinct voice. Angelic giggled and I put my hand on my jet-black, slicked-back hair, wondering what he meant by that.

Norman walked us into the pool hall and let the boys know that Angelic was always welcome there. As time went on, Norman would always talk about how we came to him with this request. The letter Angelic wrote would remain a keepsake that he held on to his entire life and every time I saw him, he'd always ask me about her and follow it by saying, "And his hair was perfect." While I never quite figured out what he meant by saying that, it brought a smile to my face every time.

As teenagers, we are all trying to make our way and develop our reputation, our character. As summer rolled around, I was preparing for high school, and having so much fun. In the mornings, I would go to conditioning with the football team, and afterwards, I'd go play golf. That was the summer I really focused on my golf game.

Artie and I and a group of our friends decided to go to a golf camp at Seven Springs Resort called the Tri State PGA Junior Golf Academy. To be fair, Artie was a much better golfer than me at this point. But when I showed up and was able to hit the ball and make my way around the course in a very respectable manner, it garnered a lot of attention. The academy was led by Bob Collins, a PGA professional. He worked with me over those few days and really got me going as a golfer. I was so proud of the trophy I took home from camp as the most improved player.

In the following weeks, I started scoring in the 90s on a regular basis and even broke 90 once in a while that summer. I'll
never forget playing in my first Junior PGA Golf Tournament
at Tam O'Shanter Golf Course and having a great showing
It made headlines; the paper featured an article that was titled
"Comeback of a Lifetime."

That summer, GeGe and Socket Head moved to Hilton Head
Island in South Carolina to make money between semesters
of college. My dad also got a job working in Pittsburgh, so two
of my biggest motivators were no longer with me every day.
The thing motivating me most now was competition.

Here in New Castle, people become legends during their high
school football careers. To this day, there are guys who are still
spoken of reverently decades after their football careers have
ended. Football is like a religion in this town, and Coach Lindy
Lauro might as well have been the pope. He commanded that
kind of authority and respect.

In the summers leading up to my freshman year, I would watch
the New Castle High School football team work out at Taggart
Stadium, not far from my home. In the heat of the Western
Pennsylvania summer sun, Coach Lauro worked his players
to exhaustion. He believed in preparation, and he wanted his
players to match the tenacity and toughness that were the
hallmarks of this town. Fact is, Coach Lauro built boys into
men, the type of men who would go on to work tirelessly in the
steel mills and others who would become leaders in medicine,
business, and politics. Coach built winners, not just on the
football field, but people who learned how to win in life.

The summer before my freshman year at New Castle High,
I couldn't wait to be one of those players grinding in the

oppressive 90-degree heat. Even though I was improving rapidly at golf, my dream had always been to play meaningful games under the lights in Taggart Stadium—the place that helped define the history of New Castle. I felt like I wouldn't have fully healed from my injuries until I made it back on that field. I needed to hear my name over the PA system when I made a tackle. I needed to hear Kenny Lebovie shout my name on the radio after a great play. I needed to carry on the Razzano football legacy in New Castle. So when Coach Lauro had his returning players working on their strength and conditioning in the summer heat, I was determined to be a part of that group.

Physically, I was nearing the end of my surgical procedures. I was beginning to move better. I was growing into myself. Playing pickup football with my friends had become a medicine to help my recovery. But pickup football was a much tamer animal than playing high school football at the New Castle Red Hurricane level. If I was going to play, it wasn't good enough to be "normal." I had to get stronger to keep up with the physicality and intensity of a higher caliber of tackle football. That meant hitting the weights harder than ever before, even harder than I did for my rehabilitation.

The weight room behind Taggart Stadium may not have been that far from my house, but it was a world away from the health club down the street where I exercised. The bare-boned concrete room didn't have the Nautilus machines of a modern-day gym. It was filled with iron barbells and dumbbells seasoned by the sweat and tears of those players that came before me. In addition to working harder than ever, I was going to have to adapt to a new way of training.

Without my left hand, training with barbells was nearly impossible. Under normal circumstances, if you were bench-pressing heavy weight, you'd need a spotter to make sure your arms don't give out and you don't drop the weight on your chest. Not being able to grip the bar with both hands made it even more of a dangerous pursuit.

Dad, always ready to encourage and push me, was able to order me a contraption that slid onto the end of my left arm and allowed me to hook the bar in. It worked well enough, but after a while, I figured out that I could rest the bar in the groove on my left hand, almost where I rested the golf club. Eventually, I wouldn't need the contraption. I found a way. There's always a way. And once I learned how to do it, I started getting stronger.

Every morning that summer, my teammates and I would meet at the stadium for conditioning. During your freshman season, anyone who wants to play can be on the team, but not everyone gets to play. And it is generally a war of attrition that keeps the better kids on the team and encourages the kids who aren't serious about it to stay home. Coach had us arrive ready at 9 a.m. and you had better be prepared to run, lift, and move like you never had before. After stretching out, the team would start with a fast-paced half-mile run around the track. We'd then run sprints: ten 100-yard sprints, eight 80s, six 60s, and so on. There was no slacking, and there wasn't much time between sprints. If you weren't giving it your all, the older guys would chew you out just as much as Coach. It was not uncommon to throw up between runs. We'd follow up our sprints by running the stadium stairs, running the hill by the student section, and then hitting agility drills for 45 minutes of nonstop action. The conditioning was amazing, and the training was extraordinary. With every step you took, you knew you were walking in the footprints of the greats who came before you and that alone made it worth it.

Most afternoons, I'd play golf before we headed back to Taggart for 6 p.m. practices where the coaches taught us the positions we'd play and installed our offensive and defensive schemes. There was a freshmen group on one side of the field and varsity on the other side. The camaraderie of training with your teammates created a bond that never fades.

After evening practice, a group of us would walk to Croton playground and hang out in the park. It would be me and Panella, Chibby, Brunz, Mancino, Louie Voto, and a whole host of other players and friends. Somehow, Chibby and Brunz always had a few cold beers waiting for us when we arrived at the park. Yeah, we were young—about 15 at the time—but times were different back then. We'd sit in the playground with our friends and inevitably Brunz would start singing. The next thing you know, there'd be a group of us singing a cappella. We were actually a pretty harmonic group. We'd sing Motown classics as we drank a few brews, always showing off for the girls. The times we had that summer were unforgettable—we worked every day together on the field and hung out every night at the playground. The friendships we built are the type that last a lifetime.

Being part of this group is what prepared me to play for the freshman football team at New Castle. It was the first step toward realizing my dream of starting for the varsity team. It was an amazing feeling to put the pads and practice jersey on for the first time.

During the very first team practice, I felt great. I made it through the individual drills and made hits in the Oklahoma drills. My confidence was soaring. We then went to a team drill. I was playing right outside linebacker and the offense ran a toss to the halfback on my side of the field. As the quarterback tossed the ball to the halfback, the guard pulled along the line of scrimmage to become one of the lead blockers on the play. I pinched down to take on the guard and try to stop the momentum of the halfback. Not having my left hand, I instinctively squared up to the pulling guard, rather than maintaining outside leverage. As I took on the guard, I forcefully shot my right hand out into his chest, trying to stand him up and move him backward toward the halfback, slowing the flow until my teammates could lend support. But in doing so, I immediately felt a jolt in my right hand. I had sprained my wrist.

When the play was over, and I went back to the defensive huddle, the pain in my wrist was excruciating. Without my left hand, I depended on my right hand for almost everything on the field. I muddled my way through the rest of the practice, knowing that I didn't play as well as I would have without the pain.

As the football season progressed, my right wrist never had a chance to heal, and I couldn't play nearly as well as I could have or should have. I was afraid to let anyone know that my wrist hurt. I didn't want to give them any excuse to say, "See, we told you that you don't belong here. You shouldn't be playing football."

As my wrist started to heal, I started making plays in practice. But the damage of my limited performance in earlier practices had been done. During one team drill, I played strong safety, and as the offense executed their running play, the running back ran counter to the flow of the offensive line. When I found myself alone with the running back, I exploded and almost knocked him out of his cleats. I was proud of the effort.

But when the play was over, I could hear the comments from the other kids to their star tailback.

"Oh man, you got blown up? By Anthony? You let Anthony do that to you?" This bothered me; I knew in my heart that I was a capable player, but no one else realized it.

My coaches had already lowered their expectations of me. I would barely make it onto the field during games. I became a feel-good story—the boy who almost died in a fire and came back to play football. To them, all that mattered was that I was there. Whether I contributed in a meaningful way or not was irrelevant. In their minds, just by being there, I had "already won."

This was a concept I just couldn't live with. It wasn't enough to wear the helmet and pads; I wanted to use them. I wanted to blow those running backs up in actual games. I knew I could do it. Now I needed a chance to show everyone else that I could. And the only way I was going to do that was to earn my way on the football field one practice at a time.

18

Gridiron

I NEVER THOUGHT of myself as a disabled kid. I always thought being disabled meant that you *couldn't* do something. In order to live the life I wanted, I convinced myself there wasn't anything I couldn't do, even without my left hand. My dad helped make sure of that.

Even before the accident, he was always a voice of encouragement. After the accident, his talks with me were relentlessly positive. He didn't believe in the word *never*.

And just as I was beginning to hit my stride with school, football, girls, life, he broke the news to me that he was moving with his new family to Pittsburgh to be closer to his new job managing a restaurant there.

It was tough enough splitting time between him and Mom. Not having them together was one of the most difficult parts of my childhood. I knew he was moving to make a living, but I couldn't help but feel rejected.

One of the loneliest memories of my life was the day he dropped me off in the alley at Mom's house and left with my younger brother Dom in the car. I stood there and watched him pull away with tears rolling down my face, not knowing when I was going to see him again. When my parents split up, my dad would say, "I didn't leave you, I left your mother." In this moment, there was no denying he left me. As I stood in the alley with a cloud of dust fresh in the air, I felt a deep loss in my heart that led to anger pulsing through me, an anger that was beginning to manifest itself in my life.

I began to use those emotions as a fuel that burned inside of me. After my disappointing freshman season, I knew I needed to work harder to forge my identity. I was learning the hard way that everything I did to survive and come back from my accident didn't mean as much in the here and now. Obviously, if I didn't fight to survive, I wouldn't be here. But there was no finish line. The fight continued every day. The further I got away from that fateful day, the more the memories faded in people's minds.

That's what I liked so much about football. All that mattered was how you played. Play well and everyone respects you. Play poorly and they don't. It was simple enough for a teenager to understand. I worked my ass off that summer in the weight room. And I ran until I couldn't run anymore, preparing for my first varsity football camp.

New Castle High School's football training camp took place every August at Sherman Acres, and it lasted two full weeks. We'd practice three times a day for five days straight, go home on the weekend, come back, and do it again for a second week. This was my first training camp and the first time I was away from home for football. And it became clear very quickly that this was serious business.

As difficult as conditioning was, Coach Lauro stepped it up a few notches at camp. Drills that are frowned on now because of player safety were considered necessary in forging a tough-ness in you that no other team could defeat. And Coach had a way of letting you know. Prior to every practice, we'd take a knee and Coach would tell us what he expected from us. Then he'd bring us together and tell us in a huddle that we were fam-ily and to look to the guys to our right and left, because these are our brothers. And we'd break the huddle by putting our hands in the middle and shouting "family" on three . . . Coach would shout out "1, 2, 3" and we'd shout FAMILY! Then we'd head off to work.

I needed this football family of mine more than anyone could realize. I was now being raised by my single mother, who was struggling to make ends meet. Between being a hairstylist and catering on the weekend, she literally had no time. My dad was gone; GeGe was living his life and not around very much. So in my young mind, this football family became all I really had. Which is the reason I gave it everything I had.

Part of Coach Lauro's toughness came from his belief in the discipline of execution. He had a play that New Castle called 28 Power. It was a running play where the ball would be given to our tailback, one of the best athletes on the team. The two guards on the offensive line would immediately vacate their position and run toward the edge of the line serving as lead blockers for the tailback who was also led by a fullback.

Coach Lauro would run that play repeatedly. "It's a perfect play," he would say. "And if we execute, we'll score a touchdown every time. They can know it's coming, but it doesn't matter, we'll just run it again!" During this camp, I was playing outside linebacker on defense. That meant it was my job to read the play, head right for the football, and try to blow up any blocker in front of the ballcarrier so that my teammates could make the tackle.

It was a thankless job. I had two linemen, at least 40 to 50 pounds bigger than I was, including my boy Shawn Panella, running full speed at me, trying to pancake me to pave a highway for the running back. Play after play after play, I threw myself into those guards without a care for my body. With every snap, I was disrupting the offense and making them better, and they were working to drive me away, which made me stronger. Exhausted, in pain, I would pick myself up off the ground and go back to the defensive huddle, knowing that the same play was coming my way again. No matter how hard it was, I just kept on fighting. Coach loved that.

At nights during camp, we were always up to something. The seniors would build a fire up by the cornfield behind the dorms and pass down stories from prior Red Hurricane teams. There was some hazing that went on, but it wasn't crazy. Some nights, Coach Lauro would join us and tell stories about prior Red Hurricane football teams. We'd listen intently to every word he said. Although we never saw it, we all knew Coach had a little whisky to go along with the hot peppers he was snacking on, as he shared some of the wisdom he gained over the years.

One night he said, "Razzano," as only he could. "I'm going to give you a piece of advice that will give you long life and prosperity. And if you do this one thing in your life, do it every day."

Well, I couldn't wait to hear his advice that was going to help unlock the success secret of life.

"What is it, Coach?" I said.

"Drink whisky and eat hot peppers," he said, and then he laughed. "Because if you do that, anything that can kill you can't live inside you!" He said it with his indescribable voice but pronounced it in a way that let you know he was kidding. He showed a bit of a grin and a smile. As players, we just laughed with him. We knew he was joking; it was a combination of our hard work and this type of levity that turned this group into a family. We worked on the field, but every one of us respected Coach like a father for the special connection he built with us off the field.

"Razzano, you know why you're so strong?" Coach asked one night during camp.

I thought he was going to talk about my toughness—my willingness in camp to take the punishment of each play.

"When I was a boy," Coach Lauro said, "I would go visit the Razzano farm in Willow Grove with my father. And your grandfather and his brothers were about the same age as me. Back in those days, the Razzanos didn't have a horse for their plow. So your grandfather and his brother Tony and his brother Pete would be strapped to the plow. And they would be dragging that farm on their backs. That's why they were so strong. Your genetics come from that. When you have to plow a farm on your back, that's the kind of strength you don't get anywhere else. They don't make 'em like you anymore, Razzano."

That camp helped to form my identity. In those two weeks, I earned the respect of my teammates and earned a spot on the junior varsity and varsity football teams. I was no longer Anthony Razzano, the nice story of the kid who almost died. I was Anthony Razzano, the linebacker/safety who was willing to do whatever it takes to win a football game. I had passed the courage test, not only with my teammates but also with Coach Lauro.

Coach Lauro had that way of lifting you up. He was an amazing speaker. We would be sitting in the locker room before a game, and Coach would always say something to command our attention.

"There's one thing that I need everyone here to learn," he said before one game. "I don't care if you're a doctor or a ditch digger. When you're asked to do a job, you do the job the best you can. You give it your all, whether you're saving a life or digging a ditch. And right now, I'm training ditch diggers." And in moments like that, you felt like you had to give the man everything you had on the field. Hard work was paramount in his world above all else. In those moments, I wasn't thinking about what my dad thought of me as a football player, or my Uncle Rick, or the people in the stands. All I cared about was what Coach Lauro thought of me.

I didn't make it on to the field a lot as a varsity player my sophomore year, but the times that I did play, it wasn't a gift. Coach Lauro didn't give gifts like that. When I earned it, he allowed me to play special teams and to get some snaps on defense at the end of games, and I took those snaps with pride. I even got to take part in New Castle's 600th victory, making us one of only a few high school teams in the United States (at that time) to reach the mark.

In our 600th victory game against Indiana, Pennsylvania, I was playing safety late in the fourth quarter. We had the contest well in hand. As a receiver was heading down the sidelines, I took my angle on him, lowered my helmet, and drilled him. I got up from the turf, fired up by my first big hit, the hit I had been dreaming about ever since I was in that West Penn Burn Unit. And then I saw the referee's yellow flag. I had hit the receiver out of bounds. Personal foul on Number 42, 15-yard penalty. Automatic first down.

After the game, I was talking to my dad when Coach Lauro walked by.

"Coach," I said. "I'm sorry about the penalty."

"I'll tell you one thing, Razzano," Coach Lauro said, putting his hand on my shoulder pads. "At least you hit him!" Coach Lauro's intensity and fire have had a profound impact on my entire life.

When I wasn't playing varsity, I was making a real impact on the junior varsity team as a starter on defense. These were the games where my personality erupted and I was as loud as can be, providing leadership on the field. I was hitting people and making things happen. I demonstrated to the coaches that I had the strength and the courage, but I still felt something was holding me back from breaking through to a starring role on the team.

I asked my position coach, Billy Humphrey, what I could do to reach that level.

"Razzano, you're everything we want in a football player," he told me. "You're tough. You're high energy. You're coachable. The only thing I'm not sure about is your mobility."

And he was right. If I had an offensive player in close space, I could crush him. But in the open field, my body wasn't allowing me to switch gears to run people down the way I should have been able to do.

As soon as the season was over, I visited Dr. Newton at West Penn to see if there was anything he could do to help me. My neck movement was so hindered, I could hardly turn my head. Without having the full range of movement in my knees and groin, I couldn't run nearly as fast as I should have.

The stiffness in my joints made it feel like I was playing in slow motion. No amount of running could make it better.

Once again, Dr. Newton put together another plan. Over the course of three weeks, he performed five surgeries on my neck, knee, and groin. Dr. Newton cut the scar tissue down to the bone in those areas. He removed it and repaired the areas microscopically with the skin and muscle from other parts of my body, requiring absolute precision to reattach the relocated arteries, veins, and capillaries.

After the nominal rehab in the hospital, I came home and did the rehab the way I knew how to do it. There was no rehab facility that was going to get me back to the field that could surpass that concrete gym at Taggart Stadium. There weren't going to be any excuses leading into my junior year. Once the fall arrived, I was going to be ready to leave everything on the field.

19

A Journey It Was

GRIEF IS SO powerful and sometimes never-ending. My mother was no stranger to it; she lost her parents, her marriage, her lifestyle, and held on through the struggle of my accident and recovery. By now, she was back on her feet, operating a catering business on the weekends and working as a hairstylist during the week. But she didn't just wake up one day recovered from her grief. She read books and shed tears and picked herself up despite her losses and moved on.

As my junior year approached, my mother could sense the pain I was harboring, the internal conflict I was dealing with. She knew that while I wore my scars well, I deeply missed having my father in my home or in town for that matter. She knew that GeGe wasn't around as much anymore as well. So, one day, she asked me what was wrong.

At the time, I didn't even know. All I knew how to do was to fight through all of the challenges and difficulties to survive, day by day, moment by moment. It was around that time that she gave me the book *The Road Less Traveled* by M. Scott Peck. "Do me a favor," she said. "Read this and tell me what you think."

And so I did. The very first line of the book said it all. "Life is difficult." It surely was. Once I picked the book up, I couldn't put it back down. I felt as though Peck's message was speaking to me. In essence, he was telling me that life was difficult for everyone. No one truly has an easy road. That book had a profound effect on my life. I started to realize that even though I had gone through so much, in reality, I wasn't that much different from everyone else. Life is difficult for everyone.

As my mindset started to change, I started to let go of some of the pain I was harboring and began to feel gratitude and happiness in a much deeper way. I concentrated on playing football to the best of my ability, fulfilling the promise I made to myself. That's what kept me going in the hospital all those months and that's what was now fueling a deeper healing in my psychological well-being.

I entered my junior year with an even greater sense of purpose and after the most recent surgical procedures, I had a newfound speed. I was still a starter on the JV team, but I was also earning more and more snaps on varsity. In fact, I became a specialist on special teams for the varsity program. If you grew up a football fan in the early 1990s, you remember Steve Tasker of the Buffalo Bills. Tasker was a special teams difference maker, perhaps the best special teams player of all time. So, while I knew I wasn't going to be a starter on defense, when Coach Lauro told me I'd be a specialist on the varsity special teams, I embraced my role. Coach would look you in the eye and tell you to be "the best you could be" and that's exactly what I did.

For anyone who knows Western Pennsylvania football, you know the rivalry between New Castle and Butler. It's legendary. Well, that year, we played Butler at Butler and the walk from our locker room to the field was particularly long. We walked to the field through one of their practice fields. Coach was leading the way as we filed in like troops behind him. The environment was incredible.

We had to kick off to open the second half; I was a gunner on the right side of the kickoff team. As the ball was received by the Butler returner, he hit a seam and it looked like he might take it the distance. Just then, I found another gear and made a touchdown-saving tackle. It was my first big play on the varsity football field. And, throughout the season, I continued to be a factor on special teams. This was a special season all the way around: I earned my first varsity letter, it was the 100-year anniversary of Red Hurricane football, and it turned out to be the final season of Coach Lauro's storied career. He retired at the end of the season. But more important than anything to me that season was the relationships I built in the locker room. I learned that football is so much more than the plays made on the field; it's a brotherhood.

One of my teammates, Stacy Scott, was a six-foot-five, 320-pound offensive lineman. We had known each other since sixth grade when we were in elementary school together. When I was held back in seventh grade, Stacy moved a year ahead of me, but now we were reconnected through football.

During camp, a group of us were talking about racism in our hometown. As we sat and talked, Stacy would talk to me about how different life was for him because he was black. I couldn't understand it.

"Stacy, we went to the same elementary school," I said. "You lived six blocks away from my dad. I've been at your house dozens of times, and you've been at my house. How much harder could you possibly have it?"

"You don't know what it's like to live in the projects," he said.

That was true. I didn't know what it was like. But Stacy's parents had a similar economic background as mine. So I wasn't convinced that he understood what life was like in the projects either. But soon, I would find out how wrong I was.

One day, after football season ended, Stacy and I were in the lunch line when he told me that his mother was thinking of sending him to Philadelphia to live with his aunt.

"It's too dangerous here, man," he said.

"Too dangerous?" I looked at him, confused. "Are you serious?"

That night, Stacy was supposed to head to Orlando as part of a group that was supporting our girls competing in the national cheerleading competition, but he never went. We would soon find out why: he was brutally murdered. His murder appeared to be a hate crime, driven by his race.

A few days later, I was at his wake. There he was, my friend, lying in an open casket, wearing his New Castle football jersey and his letterman jacket. I couldn't help but think that just a few years ago, I was the one who was supposed to be lying in that casket. It would have been Stacy coming to see me. The whole town was in mourning.

It wasn't until Stacy died that I learned about what race really meant. We could have the same backgrounds, grow up in the same place, even wear the same clothes, and I never felt like I was in danger because of the way I looked. Stacy felt like he was constantly in danger, and he was right. It was football that brought us together and made us feel like brothers. But once we stepped off that field and back into the real world, that letterman jacket couldn't protect Stacy from what life was like for him.

As it turned out, our football team wasn't the only New Castle sports program getting attention in town. Our basketball team had an incredible year, making it all the way to the semifinals of the Pennsylvania state championship, and I was one of their biggest supporters.

When basketball season ended, the school took a photo of all the basketball players wearing tuxedos to celebrate their successful season. Z, the kid who was with me in the garage on the day of my accident, was featured in the picture. Z had turned into an exceptional basketball player and was getting a lot of attention for it.

One night that junior year, after our seasons were over, we were at a party at our friend Billy's house. Billy's house was the place to hang out, and we all spent a lot of time there. On this particular night, Z was walking around with a cane acting like a big shot. Every time he walked by me, he would try to intimidate me by telling me he was going to kick my ass. He did it a few times, and I shrugged him off. I thought it was a joke. But he wouldn't stop. Then he whispered something to me.

"I'm gonna crack you with this cane," he said.

And it set me off in the middle of the party. I pushed him and said, "You're gonna kick my ass? You're gonna hit me with that cane? What do you think is going to happen? You set me on fire, and I'm still standing. You couldn't stop me then. What makes you think you can stop me now?" In all reality, I couldn't remember exactly how the fire started. These words just came out.

The entire party went silent as Billy came rushing over.

"Ant, Ant, Ant . . . ," he said. "C'mon, man, let's take a break outside."

Z was stammering for words. I pressed him. "I know you lit the match, and I never said a word to you and now you are going to try to push me around?" As he stumbled over his words, all he could do was apologize and hang his head. I told him never dare speak to me like that again. He didn't. I don't know how these words just rolled off my tongue the way they did. But, for both of our sakes, I'm glad it happened. I know he didn't mean for me to get injured the way I did, but as my friend, it had to bother him. We never talked about the fire before that, but this put an end to it.

When I look back on that night, this confrontation brought me the closure I needed to move on. It actually helped me to forgive him, which, as difficult as it may sound, was exactly what I needed to do, for my own well-being. I said what I had to say, and now it was time to look forward to my senior year. It was time to let go of the past and work toward a brighter future.

New Castle football was also looking to the future. Coach Nick Rapone took over the program and things were sure to change. Most everyone associated with the school could barely remember what the program was like before Coach Lauro. He *was* New Castle football. And now, Coach Rapone had to make the program his own.

I worked harder than ever in the summer camp leading up to my senior season. And I will never forget the day Coach Rapone came to me and told me that when we opened the season at home against Ambridge, I was going to be a starting linebacker/defensive end for the team.

At that moment, all the pain, all the surgeries, all the rehab, all the punishing summer training camps, all the weightlifting, it all paid off. I couldn't help but think back to those days in the hospital, when people would come to my room, not sure if they would ever see me alive again, and tell me, "Don't worry, Anthony. You'll be back on the field before you know it." I know they hoped for it. But I never really felt like they believed it. I wasn't even sure if I believed it myself at the time.

When that first Friday night in September came, and the lights were on at Taggart Stadium, I stood in the runway with my defensive teammates, waiting to be one of the 11 players to have their name and number called and to run on the field, as the filled stands cheered.

I heard my name and number, and I sprinted out onto the center of the field. As the national anthem played over the loudspeakers and the crowd took off their hats and showed their reverence, I thought about what it must have been like there on October 31, 1987, the day I almost died—the day that people stood in those bleachers and wept for me. I was overcome with emotion.

On this day, my first as a starter, I felt the love and perhaps miraculous disbelief from everyone in the stands. My mom, dad, and family were there, Norman Moses, Buff, Red, and the boys from the 12 o'clock crew were there. Many of the people who marched to St. Vitus to say a rosary for me the night of the accident were there. So while I was filled with emotion, I wasn't the only person in the stadium in tears. Chasing this moment is what helped keep me alive, and I survived to experience it.

To say this was the greatest game of my career would not be an understatement. I had two QB sacks in the game. But my favorite memory came with time expiring in the first half of the game. Ambridge had the ball on their 40-yard line, and they decided to run a play called Power, the same play that Coach Lauro ran over and over and over again. On this particular play, the tailback managed to squeeze through our line, and he was off and running toward our end zone. I spun off my block in pursuit. And as the tailback got into the clear with an unimpeded path to the goal, I chased him down with a diving tackle at the five-yard line as time ran out in the half.

We went on to win that night, and the play I had was a big reason why. Later that week, Coach Rapone did his weekly radio show with Kenny Lebovie and talked about that play. Listening to my coach and Kenny Lebovie talk about me on the radio was a thrill.

It wasn't the easiest season. Truth be told, that would be the only game we won that year. But I wouldn't trade that season for anything in the world, especially Senior Night. I got to walk out onto the field arm in arm with Mom and Dad to a filled stadium. I could see GeGe in the stands applauding wildly, cheering as loud as he could for me. It was an emotional moment for all of us—one of the most special moments we ever had together as a family.

Our final game was a road game against one of our rivals, Fox Chapel. As the game ended, I can remember going into the locker room and realizing that this was probably the last time I was ever going to put on shoulder pads and a helmet again. A lot of us came to the same realization. And as we sat there resting our backs against the lockers, we reflected on it all, the journey. And what a journey it was. Just as I did on opening night, I reflected, sad that it was over, but grateful that it happened, that God gave me a chance to be here, and I was able to make the most of that opportunity.

The team manager had to nudge us to get on the bus because we didn't want to leave. As a team, we rode home together one last time, and not a word was spoken the entire trip. It didn't need to be. After everything we had been through together as a team, we knew it had to end sometime, but we just wanted it to last for a moment longer. Eventually, the bus arrived back in town, and I came to the realization that now that I had achieved my dream, a dream that literally kept me alive, that dream was over.

The bus door opened, and with helmet and shoulder pads in hand, I stepped onto the pavement on a blustery New Castle night. Before my accident, I used to look at the stars in the darkness on nights like this and wonder about what my future held. It all seemed so far away. And tonight, I couldn't help but feel that the future had arrived. It was time for new goals and dreams, things that would keep me alive for the years to come. There were so many stars in the sky, and so many dreams left to make a reality.

20

Reflections

THINKING BACK ON my football career, I realize that I was not the most prolific high school football player to wear the Red Hurricane uniform. I didn't score the most touchdowns or make the most tackles. But, when it comes to the effort I put in on the football field and the work I had to do just to get the *chance* to be there—I would put *that* up against anyone. Razzanos were always known as the hardest workers on the field. And, by the grace of God, I proudly carried that legacy forward.

After my senior season, people took notice of how rare my accomplishments were and I was fortunate enough to receive many noteworthy and prestigious awards. Receiving all of this recognition was not something I expected, but my family and I were humbled and honored to be recognized in this manner.

In October of my senior year, I was selected as the recipient of the St. Francis Health Foundation Courage to Comeback Award where I was honored at a banquet of the "Who's Who" in Pittsburgh and given the opportunity to speak in front of 1,000 or more people at the Sheraton Pittsburgh Hotel at Station Square in Downtown Pittsburgh. Then, St. Francis Hospital of New Castle created the Salute to Courage Award and celebrated my achievements in front of a crowd of over 500 at a local banquet facility. The honors kept coming as I was awarded special recognition by the Lawrence County Sports Hall of Fame and given a Courage in Sports Award on the ice by the Pittsburgh Penguins later that year.

Beyond these awards, in many ways football saved my life. Being an athlete is more than just scoring touchdowns; it's about building yourself as a human being. Your statistics stay in the past. Your work ethic, competitiveness, energy, and ability to overcome adversity are what help to create your future. I needed to take the lessons I learned on the field and apply them to a new set of dreams in hopes of becoming the person I was intended to be.

However, once I accomplished my goal and my playing days were over, I was left with an empty feeling. I questioned myself: *Where do I go from here?* Perhaps for some people, there's an easy transition from the athletic field to the classroom, but not for me. So, I began searching in a different way. I started reading books written by authors like Tony Robbins, Stephen Covey, M. Scott Peck, and Zig Ziglar. I joined a direct sales company named ACN and started connecting the dots between sales success and success in recovering from my injuries. I realized that the focus, determination, and relentless pursuit of my athletic dreams could be redirected toward achieving my goals in business and as a leader in the boardroom. I went to college and earned a degree in finance and a master's degree in taxation. Along the way I met the girl of my dreams, Katie, and was lucky enough to marry her. Together, we had the goal of starting a family.

Today, I am a certified public accountant, investment advisor, and a certified NFL contract advisor. I don't dwell on all that I suffered because I'm so thankful for the many blessings in my life. I feel so lucky to have a beautiful wife of 24 years and two amazing children—Anthony Jr. and Julia—whom I love more than life itself. It wasn't easy though, and I still have plenty of difficult moments. But, once it clicked for me that I survived and made it back on the football field after being given a 0% chance to live and being given my last rites three times, every obstacle I was faced with in business and in life went from a mountain to a molehill. Yes, I've been knocked down many times, none of which compare to the moment after the fire was put out by Henry Hartman and I looked into his eyes and asked if I was going to die.

So, this isn't just a football story; it's a story about *life*. Had I not fought to survive and make it to the football field, none of this would have been possible. After my accident, my desire to play football was my true north. It was the light that guided me out of the darkness. We all have these needs or emotions that drive us. For some it's their children, for others it's their career, and for even more still, it may be the pursuit of an athletic dream or building a business. In my case, the precise moment when I realized my focus and became determined to succeed regardless of the obstacle was when I was on my back, fighting to survive.

At times, life can be overwhelming and it can seem unfair. Each stage of my life has come with its own significant challenges but, in each case, the lessons I learned from surviving my accident and making it back to the football field served as a guide for how to overcome those obstacles. You may feel that my situation is unique—unrelatable, even—but what I've realized is that *we all* face obstacles that we have to overcome in our lives. Sometimes our challenges can be life-threatening, and sometimes they are self-imposed barriers of the mind. Regardless of what you face, I truly believe that what I've learned on my journey can help you along the way and show you how to become the person *you were meant to be*.

Sometimes the obstacles in your life will knock you to the ground. It's in those moments that you have to dig deep, trust God, and allow yourself time to heal. Some battles are so intense that you'll wear scars forever, but know in your heart that even with those scars, you will smile again.

There have been many times in business when I felt like I was in a hopeless situation, but I don't let that stop me. Instead, I use those moments to reflect on the following basic principles.

Your Beliefs Will Determine Whether or Not You Are Successful

My experience taught me many lessons at a young age, but the recurring theme is that the only failure to be had in life was *not to try at all*. In order to survive, I had to adapt. I had to work harder than I ever had before. Most important, though, I had to firmly *believe* that I was going to make it.

Every day, people accomplish amazing things because their *purpose* is far more important to them than the odds of their success. It's their self-belief that enables them to defy the odds. Though you may not feel that you were born with that level of self-confidence, I'm alive today and here to tell you that thoughts are incredibly powerful. If you believe that you will *never* overcome the obstacles you face in your life or achieve the things that you want, then you won't. You'll talk yourself out of even trying if all you do is focus on how likely you are to fail. If you believe that you *can* overcome those obstacles and achieve extraordinary things, you will! Once you learn that setting high standards for yourself will allow you to overcome any obstacle, you will never settle for less again.

Your actions and decisions will follow your thoughts and beliefs, so always start with a sturdy foundation.

Success Isn't a Lonely Endeavor

If we are going to succeed in life, we all need a support system of people who've done it before. Those who achieve extraordinary things have a team of people lending their time, expertise, and energy toward the higher purpose. My survival team started with my mom and dad. Their faith in my survival never wavered. Then, we were fortunate enough to be sent to West Penn Hospital and cared for by the best burn care team in the world. Once the doctors saw that I was not going to give up, they became my greatest allies. They had the expertise to look at the most recent studies and experimental procedures. Working as a team, my chances for survival became much greater. I also had an incredible family and community who prayed to God for my survival as well as coaches, teammates, and friends who encouraged me to believe I could do anything I put my mind to.

The same is true for you, in your business and in your life. When it comes to selecting the very best teammates, don't sell yourself short. If you want to succeed you have to surround yourself with experts who can show you the way, people who are smarter than you and wish to encourage you and help you get to where you need to be. Do not surround yourself with people who refuse to challenge you or are afraid to tell you when you're headed in the wrong direction. You may think someone might be too important or successful to have the time to help you. They may seem too far out of reach. Make the effort. You have nothing to lose and everything to gain. Show them *why* you believe you are the person who will succeed. People who believe in themselves have a contagious energy; your teammates will benefit from you as you will benefit from them.

You Are Not Going to Wander Your Way to Victory; Embrace Your Setback and Make a Plan to Overcome It

If you want to do something special or achieve something new, you must not take shortcuts. You have to put in the work. No matter what the obstacle you are faced with may be, you have to identify and define what is holding you back. Your problem may not be life-threatening as mine was, but it doesn't make it any less of an adversary.

Even though I knew in my heart that I was going to survive and play football, I never could have imagined that the plan to do this would have involved cadaver skin transplants, 134 units of blood transfusions, more surgical procedures than I can count, and *years* of rehabilitation. My team of doctors engineered a plan to help me get to where I wanted to go, but it was truly up to *me* to follow that plan with everything I had. I couldn't succeed without their strategy, but their plan couldn't succeed without me. Once I was back on my feet, I had to realize that, if I wanted to get back on the field, it was going to take extraordinary dedication, planning, and persistence. I could've just denied the notion that my path to the ball field was different than the path most kids have to take, but I didn't do that. I realized that if I were going to get there, it would take extraordinary effort and commitment to a plan that met me where I was while challenging me to reach my potential. Later in life, I realized that, to achieve success in the classroom and in business, I had to be willing to feel the pain of handling my work, studying, and challenging myself intellectually all over again. I had to discipline myself to meet deadlines, show up to the office, build relationships, and hammer out every job given to me in order to achieve success.

Too often, people live in denial that a problem even exists, and therefore they cannot possibly resolve it. On the day of my accident, I asked if I could play football that very night, because I didn't want to believe what had happened. I truly believe that, had I stayed in that mindset, I wouldn't have made it to where I am today; perhaps I wouldn't have made it at all. The truth is, in order to succeed, you have to have an open mind and acknowledge what is holding you back.

- Are you in the wrong market?
- Are your employees capable of doing their jobs?
- Is your product better than your competitors?
- Are you properly capitalized?
- Are *you* willing to do what it takes?

Only when you are brutally honest with yourself about who you are, what you want, and how you're going to get there will you make the necessary commitments to become the person you want to be.

If you want something in life, you have to be willing to go through the pains of hard work to achieve it. Sometimes that means taking a path less traveled, but it's better to forge your own way with clarity than to live in smoke and mirrors having never taken your first step.

Gratitude Is the Key

Through it all, if I could live my life all over, I wouldn't change a thing: not my parents' divorce, not going through the fire— none of it. I'd choose every surgery, every blood transfusion, and even the loss of my left hand all over again. I know it sounds crazy, but I'm so grateful for these life experiences.

They made me who I am today. Now, I get to share all these lessons with you, and hopefully you will begin to see every struggle in your life as a blessing.

Does that mean that there will be no tears? No, hardship is still hardship, even when you have the grit to endure it.

Does it mean you should love disappointment and suffering? Of course not, but you should be able to find the blessing in them. It's okay to feel bad sometimes; we are all going to shed tears. But don't live there and, by all means, *don't* feel sorry for yourself. Look for the strength; sometimes you'll find it within and oftentimes it will come from another human being.

When you reach the other side of the struggle, you will hardly remember the pain, but you will have gained the confidence to do whatever it is that you set your mind to. And, in that moment, you will be thankful for all the blood, sweat, and tears it took to get there. That's what *living* is; that's what the human experience is all about and what makes each of us so unique. Whether or not you achieve great financial success, you'll always be able to look back at your life and say *I did it!*

Finally, the Most Important Lesson Is This: *Don't Ever Let a Setback Define Who You Are*

Most people believe that success comes from putting in time and, therefore, expect results. The reality is, as M. Scott Peck so eloquently states, "life is difficult and so is business." There isn't always a correlation between effort and results; success just doesn't always happen according to our plan.

Too often, we allow the things that hold us back to define us. We accept our limiting beliefs as the truth of who we are. In reality, it's not the setback that defines you, but how you respond to each setback that determines *who you become*. This is the most critical part of the journey: instead of allowing your obstacle to define you, you must define your obstacle so you can overcome it.

We can't get stuck in the mindset of questioning *why* our situation is difficult or stuck in the frustration that we didn't *deserve* to encounter a particular problem. We have to be resolved in our understanding that success is a difficult undertaking and focused on achievement regardless of what we are faced with. The best way to overcome adversity or to make it through a crisis is to quit asking yourself, *why me?* Accept that the problem exists and immediately begin asking yourself, *how do I get through this?* When we look at it this way, we quit wasting time on anger or resentment in a difficult situation and begin focusing on the results we are looking for and how we are going to get there.

Successful people fail all the time. The only difference is they do not let that failure define who they are or, more important, who they can grow to be. They know that any moment can be the instant that you change your life forever—for better or for worse—and that success is all about solving life's difficult problems.

In my life, my goal was to play football under the lights at Taggart Stadium. I could have given up on that dream, but I didn't. I made the conscious choice to define my own abilities, to seize my destiny and change the trajectory of my life after the accident that almost ended it all. I know that *you* have the ability to change your life, too; the moment you make that conscious decision to stop defining yourself by your setbacks and instead define yourself by your potential to overcome is the moment you *truly* start to live.

And finally, in the words of Saint John Paul II, "I plead with you! Never, ever give up on hope, never doubt, never tire, and never become discouraged. Be not afraid." In the end it doesn't matter what your endeavor is or the role you play in it; give it all you got, be thankful to God, and let the goodness of his Glory shine through you—now and forever!

Amen.

21

Photo Gallery

1983. Family portrait. From left, Dad, Mom, Ge-Ge, Anthony.

1983. Dad and me at a Pirates game.

1985. Winning the Memorial Day Championship. Baseball was my first love!

1987. Pop Warner Football, North Hill Redskins.

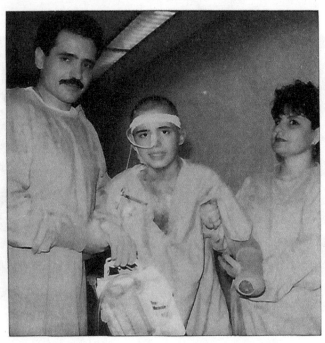

1987. My first steps after the accident. Probably the most powerful picture I have! Never forget where you come from!

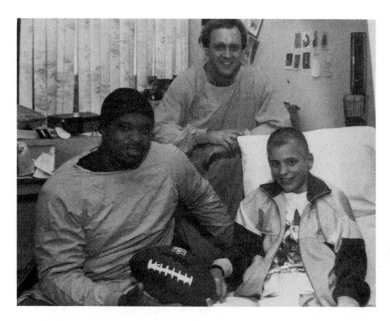

1987. From left: Pittsburgh Steeler Edmund Nelson, KDKA news anchor Jon Burnett, and me. Always great to be visited by a pro athlete!

1987. Great picture of the team at the West Penn Burn Unit who saved my life! (I wish I could remember everyone's name.)

January 26, 1988. My friends welcoming me home from the hospital. From left: Brian Grebenz, me, Artie Flamino, Todd Tropea, and Mikey Porada (RIP).

June 1988. Burn Camp!

July 1988. Our Ocean City trip!

1989. Headed to the eighth-grade prom.

November 1988. From left: Mom, me, and Dad at the American Legion Courage Award dinner.

1993. Senior night with Dad.

1993. Home opener against Ambridge. Running off the field to greet Coach Rapone after making a QB sack.

1993. Salute to Courage Award, New Castle, Pennsylvania. From left: me, Grandpa John Razzano, and Sister Donna Zwigert of the St. Francis Health Foundation.

1994. Courage to Comeback Award dinner, Pittsburgh, Pennsylvania. Rocky Bleier and me with other award recipients and attendees.

1994. Pittsburgh Penguins Courage in Sports Award, talking with Rick Tocchet, Pittsburgh Penguins.

April 24, 1999. Katie and I married. Father Mauro married us. He also gave me my last rites in the West Penn Burn Unit.

June 2002. From left: Dad, my daughter Julia, me, and Mom at Julia's baptism.

May 2004. Julia gives me a smooch to congratulate me on my master's degree.

July 2008. Giving the pregame speech as president/GM of New Castle Thunder Minor League Football Team!

April 2009. Celebrating the 40-year anniversary of the West Penn Burn Unit with Dr. Goldfarb.

2010. Dinner with Henry Hartmann.

December 2011. Welcoming our son Anthony into the world! From left: Anthony, Katie, Julia, and me.

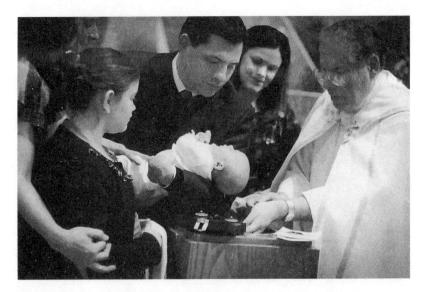

February 2012. Anthony's baptism. Angelic is his godmother with Father Ben performing the baptism. Father Ben also gave me my last rites while I was in the burn unit.

August 2013. Award from Jet Blue at the North American One-Armed Golf Association National Championship at the PGA National Golf Club in Florida.

January 2015. Mom and me on her birthday.

September 2016. Hanging with the boys from our pool-shooting days at Norman Moses's garage. From left: Johnny Frank, Artie Flamino, Danny DePaolo, me, Adam Ginnochi, and Michael Liberatore.

March 2016. Speaking engagement, Flash Point Communications, Costa Mesa, California.

September 2016. Talking to a class at St. Vitus Elementary School.

June 2017. Me and the kids visiting Burn Camp as a survivor. Hanging in the bubbles with the fire trucks behind us.

September 22, 2017. Visiting the healing water at Lourdes, France. Our family came together after each of us were submerged in the healing water.

October 31, 2017. Hosted a blood drive with the American Red Cross to recognize the 30-year anniversary of the fire.

2018. Visiting the West Penn Burn Unit. Me and my primary nurse Linda Leonard. Honored that my picture was still on the wall!

2019. Serving Mass at the Church of Our Lady of Victories, also referred to as the Shrine of the Infant Jesus of Prague with my son, Anthony. The Mass was celebrated by Father Joe Luisi, who also administered my last rites in the burn unit.

2020. Coaching my son and his team to a Tournament of Champions victory. Life has gone full circle!

2022. Anthony's first out-of-the-park home run! That's him and Coach Nick Benson! So great to see my boy succeed at baseball!!

2023. Anthony and me in the batting cages getting it done!

2022. Julia and me on a father-daughter date in Pittsburgh!

2023. Uncle Rick and me coaching Anthony's flag football team!
And check out the handsome young man in the back row pointing
at the camera. That's Nick Nesser, my favorite cousin Kristen's son!
Family is everything!

2023. Katie and me shopping in an Italian deli to prepare a traditional Sunday dinner for our family!! Sauce and meatballs!

2023. Me reflecting on this awesome journey as I gaze down the cobblestone road at the original St. Vitus Cathedral in Prague.

About the Author

AT THE AGE of 12, Anthony Razzano followed the script of many young boys. He wanted to play football, and on the evening of October 31, 1987, he was scheduled to play in an important Pop Warner football game under the lights at the historic Taggart Stadium. However, on that day, the script changed tragically. At the flick of a match in his family's garage, a catastrophic incident forced Anthony out a side door, engulfed in a ball of flames. Neighbors acted quickly to extinguish the fire and summon paramedics who rushed him to a nearby hospital.

Anthony was transported by helicopter to one of the top burn trauma centers in the country, the West Penn Burn Unit in Pittsburgh, Pennsylvania. While the medical staff worked to save his life, the doctors drove home the seriousness of the situation to his family. His family was told to make funeral arrangements. The doctors said they would do everything in their power to save his life, but they did not give any hope for him to survive.

However, after battling multiple bouts of sepsis, more than 134 blood transfusions, and being given his last rights three times, remarkably, Anthony survived and was released from the hospital on January 14, 1988. When Anthony walked out of West Penn, he didn't walk alone. With his family by his side and halls lined with patients, medical staff, and members of the media applauding, he beat the odds.

But surviving wasn't enough for Anthony. With fierce determination he persevered through the painful recovery, the intense physical therapy, and every other obstacle in his way to live a meaningful life. Although he lost the fingers on his left hand and suffered scarring all over his body, he continued to fight back and ultimately resumed playing football for the New Castle Red Hurricanes. In fact, again defying the odds, Anthony was a two-year letterman on the varsity football team and starting outside linebacker his senior year. Ultimately realizing his dream of playing under the lights at Taggart Stadium. Anthony knows his survival was a blessing from God. He believes he was blessed with this miraculous recovery to inspire others to keep fighting when they are hardest hit.

Anthony continues to use the lessons he learned through this tragedy to achieve new goals. He went on to earn a bachelor's of science in business administration and a master of science in taxation. Today, Anthony is a certified public accountant and a certified NFL contract advisor. He and his wife Katie of 24 years have operated their own business advisory firm for 18 years. They are the parents of two amazing children, Julia, 20, and Anthony Jr., 11. Anthony Sr, can often be found volunteering as a youth coach on baseball and football fields, where he teaches young people the power of perseverance.

Acknowledgments

Writing this book was much harder than I ever expected and there's no way I could have done it without an amazing support system and incredible people who inspire me.

First, and foremost, I have to give credit to God, the Father, Son, and Holy Spirit. Three people, one God. I know, in my heart that it is you who saved me. And I know that each of the words written in this book come from you, not from me. Thank you, God, for loving me when I wasn't loveable. For healing me, when it seemed impossible, and for giving me the strength to carry on when there was no hope. I love you and know that this book and my life would not be possible without your grace and mercy.

My wife, Katie. I don't know if I could ever thank you enough for putting up with me. Even though we were just kids when we met, I know your love healed parts of my soul that no one will ever see. You're special, Little Tuffy! This book, our business, and our family doesn't work without you!! I love you!!

My beloved daughter, Julia. Remember when we were sitting in Ocean City and prayed that one day there would be a movie made about this life's journey? Well, that moment inspired me to start this and I couldn't have written this book without you! You're special, baby girl! I love you!

My son, Anthony Jr. Every day when we go to the ball field I look at you, I see myself, and it takes me back to the days before I was burned. Being your dad has helped me remember life before the fire and I'm really thankful for you giving me that feeling back in my life. I love you!

Mom and Dad. You both had a really hard job. Thank you for keeping all of the records, the calendar, and all of the newspaper articles. They were invaluable in this process! I love you both!!

Grandpa John. Thank you so much for being my advocate, teaching me how to write, and the art of public speaking. May God continue to bless you and Grandma in heaven!

Uncle Rick and Jill. Thank you for being among the first to read this. Your input was invaluable. God bless you both.

Father Joe Luisi and the one and only Leslie Sansone. It was mid-August 2019, and we were on a pilgrimage visiting Eastern Europe, sitting in a hotel lobby in Prague when I shared my thoughts of writing this book. Thank you for inspiring me to write this. Your influence led me to this and for that I am forever thankful!

Chibby. While I was writing this you were by my side every day. You reminded me of memories of our childhood and were so proud of me for writing this. I can't believe you died before it was published. I love you, brother. I pray for you and will do my best for your family. Please pray for us!

Andrew. Thank you for being the first person to read my manuscript. Your thoughts and ideas were instrumental in bringing this book to life!

My friends Artie Todd Tropea, Angelic, and Raelynn. I'd call you while I was writing this book and pick your brain about growing up. Thank you for refreshing my memories!! You guys are the best!

Special thank you to the *New Castle News*, Rocky Bleier, Liz Miles, Mark Malone, and every other member of the media who documented my story in both written and video production. Without your amazing coverage of my life, this book would not have been possible!

Thank you Linda Leonard, my primary nurse at West Penn, for taking the time to talk with me and our team as we wrote this book!! You were there through the dressing changes, my first steps, and even my first day back to school. But, my favorite memory is you calming my dad when he thought I was dying from an excessively loud and long "breaking of the wind" after surgery!! We still laugh about that!!

Thank you to all of my doctors, nurses, and medical professionals who saved my life. Who would have known that your work was not only saving a life but also providing material for writing this book. You are real-life superheroes!

My teachers and coaches at the New Castle Area School District. Thank you so much for teaching me, helping me grow as a person, and never making me feel less than!! I love you and know in my heart, that my achievements in life are not possible without you all! We are N.C.! We are N.C.!

My teachers and mentors at Robert Morris University. You are the best of the best. I owe you so much, especially for instituting a tremendous communications program for business majors. It's this basis that provided me the foundation for public speaking and writing this book!

Thank you to Kevin Anderson and Associates for guiding me through this process as a first-time author, especially Ian Corson and Amanda Ayers Barnett. Ian, you believed in me and my ability to write this before I did. Thank you for following through. I wouldn't have finished the book without you! And Amanda, your attention to detail as a senior editor provided invaluable feedback to this process!

But look, if you don't know who Michael Dolan is, find out. Michael worked closely with me for 15 months as an expert helping me outline, structure, document, write, and rewrite again. While I told the story and put it to word, you were amazing!! You listened to me cry while writing and those moments allowed me to process all that I went through in a much more significant way than you'll ever know! This book doesn't get finished without you, my friend. Thank you, Miguel!

To my boy Scott Empringham and Empringham Media Group, thank you for being the most positive guy on the planet! You took the time to read my manuscript and led me to the amazing Amber Vilhauer and NGNG Enterprises. Without you both, I would have never met That Girl Charlie, TGC Worldwide!

Thank you TGC Worldwide, especially "That Girl" Charlie Fusco for your guidance, representation. and for getting this first-time author published through Wiley!! I know how hard you, John Michael Esposito, and your entire team worked to make this happen. You're a true visionary who can work with anyone you choose. Thank you for choosing me!

And thank you to our publisher, Wiley, a global leader in publishing, for taking on a little guy like me and making it possible to share my story with the world!! It is because of you, Jeanenne Ray, Jozette Moses, Michelle Hacker, and the rest of the team that we can bring this message of hope to the world, and for that I am forever grateful!!

Index

Page numbers in italics refer to photographs.